Pocket Racing Guide

The Daily Telegraph

Pocket
Racing Guide

THE INSIDE TRACK ON
HORSERACING

TONY STAFFORD

CollinsWillow
An Imprint of HarperCollins*Publishers*

First published in 1994 by
CollinsWillow
an imprint of HarperCollins*Publishers*
London

This fully revised and updated edition
published 2000

Tony Stafford 2000

1 3 5 7 9 8 6 4 2

A CIP catalogue record for this book is
available from the British Library

ISBN 0 00 218968 2

Printed and bound in Great Britain by Edinburgh Press

Dedication

For Joseph and Abigail

'One man's blinkers are another man's focus.'
Sheikh Mohammed

Contents

Foreword

There have been many changes in horseracing over the years. Since I began training about 30 years ago, many of the old-style owner-breeders have disappeared, much to my own disappointment. Many of our major wins at Warren Place originally came from home-breds, but very few individuals nowadays can afford to maintain a large breeding establishment.

At the same time the coverage of horseracing, as in many other sports, has been transformed. As coverage has increased on television and in the written media, so the intensity of the scrutiny has also heightened.

Many newspaper writers believe that a headline, which screams out at its audience, is more important than a serious interpretation of the true facts of any issue. Some of the papers and television companies forget that experience is a quality to seek in their writers and contributors.

From the time that I first became aware of Tony Stafford's writing in the *Daily Telegraph*, and more recently, since I have got to know him personally, I have come to respect the fact that he does not pursue the 'headlines at all cost' route.

Tony is someone who is very knowledgeable about many areas of racing, and adds to his knowledge, the ability to make his stories both readable and accurate at the same time. There is nothing more irritating than to speak on the telephone to a reporter, who then misquotes you in the subsequent article, usually seeking out the negative aspects of any situation.

In the old days, I came to admire the work of the late Michael Seely, who did such good work for the *Times* over many years. Mikey is sadly missed, but I regard Tony as being in a similar category, one in which very few other present-day writers can be included.

I have read much of his work, and enjoyed reading this book. It contains much of interest to those well versed in racing, and much more to inform people who at present have only a limited knowledge of the subject.

Henry Cecil
Warren Place,
Newmarket, April 2000.

Introduction

Perhaps it is simply coincidence. Maybe we are making too much of it, but at the turn of the year 2000 British horseracing is almost unrecognisable from the sport of just twenty or even ten years ago.

Change – especially in terms of the screening of races and betting on them – started gently early in the last decade of the old century and gathered apparently unstoppable momentum. The advent of spread betting, offshore developments, and application of the internet altered many preconceptions.

In the 1990s, many leading professionals departed the competitive side of the sport. Among Flat jockeys, Lester Piggott retired (again), as did Willie Carson. Pat Eddery neared the end of his career and Kieren Fallon emerged as the pre-eminent rider, with Frankie Dettori remaining the man for the big occasion.

Among trainers, the former Dubai policeman Saeed bin Suroor confounded all the sceptical critics of his appointment as trainer of the Sheikh Mohammed brainchild stable of Godolphin. He has overseen a string of Classic winners and, more importantly, exceptional performances by a series of older champions.

Henry Cecil and John Dunlop remained at the top of the tree, joined by the ever-industrious Barry Hills; but Peter Chapple-Hyam's departure from Robert Sangster's Manton showpiece brought the unexpected signing of John Gosden to leave his Newmarket stronghold. Meanwhile Dick Hern and Jack Berry were notable departures.

Less familiar names, like former northern Flat jockey David Nicholls and the little-known jump jockey Karl Burke, both showed an instant talent for training winners and a flair for the promotional side of the business. David Loder emerged as a juvenile specialist in Newmarket, but then in the winter of 1998 decamped to Evry in France to train Godolphin's younger division.

In Ireland, an even younger trainer was to transform the handling of classically bred young talent. A name like O'Brien might not seem too unusual in Ireland, except that the greatest ever racehorse trainer, Vincent, happened to possess it. His long-standing base at Ballydoyle, Co Tipperary, passed in mid-decade to his namesake, but no relation, Aidan O'Brien, training for the all-powerful Coolmore Stud team of John Magnier (Vincent's son-in-law) and partners.

In 1999, O'Brien introduced to the racecourse a string of precocious top-class juveniles. He and, more pointedly, Coolmore balanced the need for future Classic eminence with feeding the world-wide breeders' hunger for fast, young stallions. In jump racing, the Flat-race achievements of Aidan O'Brien, himself trainer of the peerless triple-Champion Hurdle winner Istabraq, were matched by the astonishing Martin Pipe/Tony McCoy trainer–jockey combination. McCoy's emergence, interestingly from the same Jim Bolger stable background that produced O'Brien, ended the championship aspirations of the talented Adrian Maguire, while Richard Dunwoody had to bring forward retirement after injury.

There was also the feeling that constantly opposing Pipe and his brilliant organisation and development of jumpers eventually discouraged and even disillusioned such long-standing training luminaries as David Nicholson and Jenny Pitman, both of whom retired in the last half of 1999. Fortunately for devotees of females in racing, the highly versatile Mary Reveley, who could win races in any code, Flat or jumping, and the brilliant newcomer Venetia Williams, pushed inexorably into the top echelon.

Pipe, the admirably consistent Nicky Henderson and another youngster Paul Nicholls all joined in the rapid development of the trade in French-bred horses, especially steeplechasers, whose early maturity brought calls for more drastic changes to the weight-for-age scale.

Among owners, Sheikh Mohammed and his brothers Maktoum, Hamdan and to a lesser extent Ahmed remained pre-eminent, but Magnier and his new associate, the former East End bookmaker Michael Tabor, matched them almost blow for blow.

The Saudi Arabian influence remained strong, with Prince Khalid Abdulla and his son-in-law Prince Fahd Salman both maintaining powerful stables, principally nowadays with products of their own studs. Prince Fahd's younger brother, Prince Ahmed Salman, returned from a self-imposed exile from the racing industry to develop his Thoroughbred Corporation team, principally in California, but with a strong English base. The 1999 Derby win by Oath, and major successes by both Royal Anthem and Dr Fong at the highest level, signalled Prince Ahmed's arrival in the top league. His Breeders' Cup Juvenile win for Anees in Florida in November 1999 was icing on a very sweet cake for the owner.

That race proved the big-race swansong for yet another jockey of world-wide acclaim. Gary Stevens, the outstanding jockey in the United States, gave the British racing fans a fleeting glimpse of his talent in a three-month summer stint in 1999 before leaving abruptly to become retained jockey for Prince Ahmed. That relationship was just as quickly ruptured when chronic arthritis in his right knee caused the 36-year-old's retirement.

Time will probably show, however, that all these adjustments will amount to a 'can of beans' beside the seismic shifts in other areas. The Jockey Club was replaced as the crucial authority in racing by the British Horse-racing Board, whose much-criticised but highly independent chairman Peter Savill was the ideal personality to preside over the technological revolution.

Televising of racing into betting shops in the late 1980s was the first real technological advance. Satellite Information Services' coverage was accompanied a decade later with the formation of The Racing Channel, which provided the first chance for home-based racing fans to receive regular comprehensive daily broadcasts of races.

Domestic satellite coverage also developed with Sky Sports, and at the turn of the century the latter company and Channel 4 were the front-line competitors who were exploring the possibility of harnessing the developments in digital television to enhance and greatly expand their coverage.

The future for Satellite Information Services (SIS) might seem bleak. Certainly the racecourses, owners of rights to the programmes and the pictures, were anxious to benefit from the rewards they foresaw in expanded world-wide internet broadcasting and pool betting. A fair guide to the worth of their product was news of a planned £450,000 transfer fee for a single Boxing Day race date from one minor track, Newton Abbot, to another, Towcester. Later, this planned transfer was apparently blocked by a higher authority.

It is inevitable that soon a punter in New York will be able to watch and bet on races in Britain and anywhere else in the world from an armchair. The potential rewards would match the obvious benefits that so many pioneering internet businesses derived as computers became almost as common as refrigerators.

The Racecourse Association, which represents the interests of 59 tracks, approaches the end of SIS's 10-year agreement in 2002, presiding over anything but a united stance. Representatives of the so-called 'premier league' of the 12 biggest courses agreed a comprehensive £225 million ten-year deal with Channel 4 and their junior partner the BBC in February 2000 – to maintain the coverage of those tracks on terrestrial TV rather than the option of Rupert Murdoch's BSkyB satellite empire. Some observers were sceptical that this would even be ratified, and with good reason, as ten-year deals in the internet age are like 100-year deals of earlier times. Meanwhile, some of the relative minnows – particularly Graham Parr of Arena Leisure, owners of all three existing all-weather tracks, and Stan Clarke, boss of, among others, Newcastle and Uttoxeter – were steadily adding assets and, in the case of Arena, planning their own internet operation.

Parr and Clarke, both successful in other businesses, were among the original bidders for a proposed new race-course, which would be selected from eight applicants during the spring. Parr's Arena Leisure group withdrew its bid to race from a site in Thurrock, East of London, and were thought to be backing Clarke's planned addition of an all-weather surface with floodlighting to the existing Newcastle track at Gosforth Park. Northern trainers were disappointed to hear that this plan had been rejected in favour of two entirely new tracks. One, for night dirt racing at Fairlop Waters in east London is known as London City racecourse. The other, on turf, is planned for Pembrey, South Wales.

One name, though, stands out as the supreme catalyst in many of these changes. For years, British racing has been under-funded. Whether prize money is inadequate or not, the fact remains that the government and book-makers each derive a much greater proportion of the money generated from betting on horseracing than does the sport itself. The decision of the highly respected rails bookmaker Victor Chandler to move offshore to Gibraltar and offer, via free telephone calls, a betting service with only a 3 percent 'service' deduction compared with 9 per-cent on the mainland, has transformed the marketplace. That single brave development acted as a 'king's new clothes' situation which caused a fundamental rethink, not least in government, on how to progress. Other firms followed, while several internet operators experienced excellent turnover when going live in 1999.

Soon, people who were previously happy with the status quo were actively promoting a cut of domestic betting duty to 3 percent, or even nothing in the case of the maverick John Brown of William Hill. Whatever the end-game, the life of the Levy Board – to my mind always an irrelevance and merely a costly way of racing's reshuffling the cards – must soon be at an end.

Coming back to Savill, his premise was that racing needed to receive a greater share of betting revenue. SIS has a major bookmaking element in its ownership. Interestingly, and perhaps because of that, it has been highly profitable. But then, its pricing policy has been such that relatively poor betting-shop operators have been compelled to pay to SIS the same price for their product as much richer shop owners. That has been allowed at the same time as the poorer operators have been permitted to contribute only a tiny sum to racing via the Levy. The Racecourse Association will not tolerate such unfairness even if they do agree to accept SIS proposals for a new contract. Come 2002, the new deal will be more equitable and racing will get a fairer share of the betting cake.

Time, I am sure, will show that Savill, Chandler and Lord Hartington, who presided over the transfer of power from the Jockey Club to the British Horseracing Board, will have been the three heroes who took the sport out of the nineteenth century and straight into the twenty-first. Savill's role will become even more important following the decision in March 2000 by Jack Straw, the Home Secretary, to end the Levy system of funding racing. He additionally pledged to allow the sale of the Tote to a racing consortium, the preferred option of the existing Tote Board and its innovative and intelligent chairman Peter Jones.

Straw's decisions are naturally interlinked. Only by integrating these two elements will racing be able to develop fully its potential and prosperity. Racing, in one guise or another, should control the Tote and also set the agenda for pricing the product.

CHAPTER ONE

Beginnings

Horseracing today is a well-regulated, highly organised spectator sport that lends itself readily to television coverage and attracts vast sums in betting turnover – and therefore revenue – throughout much of the world. It is easy to see why that popularity could have developed from the earliest days of civilisation.

The horse was soon identified as one of the most versatile and useful of animals. It was the basis of transportation, by horseback or carriage. It was the means by which farming could be intensified. It was also a subject of great pride, especially among rich men who would insist on acquiring the fastest and best-looking specimens of the breed.

Records of chariot races being introduced to the ancient Greek Olympic Games date as far back as 680 BC. The equine element in the Games was extended a few years later when bareback horse-riding became part of the programme, and stayed as a feature until the ancient Games moved to Rome in the last century BC.

The first recorded instance of organised horseraces in England was during the Roman occupation in 210 AD –

when Arabian horses, brought to England by the Emperor Severus Septimus, competed with the domestic animals based at the Roman encampment at Wetherby.

No doubt a forebear of Mary Reveley's trained a couple of the winners that day. It is equally probable that a long-gone member of the Barry Hills family was on hand at the first recorded race-meeting on the Roodeye. This racecourse, just outside the walls of the City of Chester, first staged races in 1540 on the identical spot where racegoers still throng with such anticipation every May.

It was later in the sixteenth century that the royal connection, which was to remain a major element in British horseracing for the rest of the millennium, was first cemented. Queen Elizabeth I was a visitor to the races on Salisbury Plain. Two later monarchs, King Charles II and Queen Anne, were largely responsible for the popularisation of racing at Newmarket and Ascot. Charles' relish for riding across Newmarket Heath culminated in his becoming the only ruling monarch ever to ride a winner, the 1671 Town Plate – a race that still exists with its time-honoured prize of several pounds of Newmarket sausages. A notable first triumph!

The Town Plate retains one unique link with the ancient formulation of racing: it is still run over three miles and six furlongs on the July course at Newmarket, a reminder of the days when four-mile heats and a run-off were the norm. The Town Plate is nowadays staged with the accompaniment of betting, on its regular Sunday date in October. No other Flat race in Britain is staged over more than two and three-quarter miles – the latter is the distance of the Queen Alexandra Stakes at Royal Ascot.

Queen Anne's chance involvement in the foundation of the Royal Ascot meeting reputedly dates from one occasion when she was riding in a carriage through Windsor Forest after a day following the Royal Buck-hounds. On arriving at a clearing known as Ascot, she realised that the vast open Heath would provide the perfect natural setting for a racecourse. A niece of King Charles II, she shared his love of riding but had long been unable to continue when she founded Ascot racecourse at the age of 46.

The first meeting was staged in the summer of that year to coincide with the arrival of the Court at Windsor, six miles from the track. Within two years the Queen had died, and her immediate successors – George I and II – had so little interest in horseracing that, for around thirty years, Ascot became neglected to the extent that there were several years when no meetings were staged.

Fortunately, however, while royal patronage declined, the horse breed was developing. Either side of the founding of Ascot, the importation of several Arab horses – subsequently to be mated with the domestic breed of hunter, which dominated racing at the time – transformed and refined the breed. By the middle of the eighteenth century the racehorse had been developed into a recognisable model of the present-day thoroughbred, with all the modifications of physical form and the combination of stamina and speed that have made the racehorse such an attraction.

Importation of the Byerley Turk in 1689, the Darley Arabian early in the new century, and the Godolphin Arabian or Barb in 1729 were the vital ingredients. The

Darley Arabian's claim to posthumous fame was his place as the great-great-grandsire of the incomparable Eclipse, winner of all his 18 races – seven of them walkovers, so reluctant were other owners to challenge him. Each time he did meet an opponent (only 20 in his entire career), he started at odds-on.

After retirement Eclipse became an outstanding stallion – although only once was he leading sire because he had to give best in other years to Herod and his son Highflyer, descendants of the Byerly Turk. Unlike the Herod line, which has largely died out, Eclipse's name lives on in the pedigrees of more than 90 percent of modern thoroughbreds, pre-eminently in the Northern Dancer dynasty. As early as 1730 another son of the Darley Arabian, Bulle Rocke, became the first thoroughbred to be exported to North America, when sent to Virginia where horseracing was becoming increasingly important.

With a fitting sense of history and the part played in it by Arabian horses, Sheikh Mohammed, Crown Prince of Dubai, called his stud operation Darley. More recently his world-wide racing operation has been called Godolphin, to celebrate the importance of those early foundation sires. Like the Sheikh, the Saudi Princes – Khalid Abdulla and Fahd and Ahmed Salman – are great students of the sport on a world scale, understanding its traditions and helping to ensure its future with thoughtful, selective breeding policies.

The next crucial date for English racing was 1750 when the Jockey Club – which would become the supreme arbiter of all racing matters – was founded at the

Star and Garter in London's Pall Mall. Within a few years the Jockey Club had passed a resolution that riders would have to 'weigh in' after races. In 1762 the registration of owners' racing colours was introduced. Development continued apace.

Before the end of the eighteenth century (1752) the first steeplechase was run in Cork in Ireland, over four and a half miles of hunting country between the steeples of Buttevant and St Leger Churches. In the same period, Richard Tattersall started the bloodstock sales company which still carries his name, from premises at Hyde Park. Two-year-old races were instigated at Newmarket, and James Weatherby – founder of the firm which still acts as today's racing administration and secretariat – published the first Racing Calendar, also still in existence today.

In the next ten years, three of the five enduring 'Classic' races were begun. The St Leger was staged at Doncaster for the first time in 1776, although it did not receive its historical name until two years later. It was a toss of a coin between Lord Derby and Sir Charles Bunbury, one of the leading lights of the turf in the last years of the century, that decided the latter's name should be attached to the Derby – a title now adorning the top race in most other racing countries. The first Derby was staged at Epsom in 1780 and was won, perhaps appropriately, by Sir Charles Bunbury's Diomed.

It was in fact at a dinner party after the previous year's successful first running of the Oaks – for three-year-old fillies, also run at Epsom – that the proposal to inaugurate a counterpart race for three-year-old colts was agreed. The popularity of both races has remained high despite some modern-day criticisms, especially in terms of the early June timing of the Derby, which some commentators regard as coming too early in the racing year.

While Flat racing was establishing a pattern, revolving as it still does around Classic races, jump racing was also developing. The first steeplechase in England was staged in Leicestershire, over an eight-mile course in 1792; and as early as 1811, the first meeting over manufactured rather than natural obstacles attracted a crowd estimated at 40,000 to the now defunct Bedford racecourse.

Rapid development of the railway network made access to race meetings in the middle of the nineteenth century easier, both for spectators and for the horses, for whom this mode of travel became the favoured means of transportation. In some cases this became the basis for a successful betting coup with an unexpected late arrival winning at long odds.

In the late 1830s the Grand National was instituted at Aintree near Liverpool, under its original title of the Grand Liverpool Steeplechase. The first winner, in 1839, was Lottery, but his fame has been largely eclipsed by that of the noted Irish rider Captain Martin Becher, whose mount Conrad deposited him into the brook which now is universally known as Becher's Brook (fence six and 22 in the modern Grand National).

Large crowds at race meetings encouraged the establishment of many more courses. The enclosed Park tracks around London – Sandown, Kempton and the much-loved Hurst Park (now sadly a housing estate) – proved a highly successful model of the modern racecourse.

In the twentieth century, tote betting – based on a

pool of all the bets, rather than the time-honoured, and in some cases dishonoured, betting with bookmakers – also provided the model for most other racing countries. In the United States, for example, tote or pari-mutuel odds were the only available prices for horserace betting. But as that century ended, internet betting, and the fixed forward odds in the big Las Vegas sports books, modified that monopoly.

Now we await the next conceptual leap – home betting and viewing via a computer, phone and digital television link into either a world-wide pari-mutuel pool or at fixed odds. The choices will be endless. Time, together with that great leveller – the means by which the various racing organisations around the world are to be funded – will help this new electronic business arrive at the optimum conclusion.

CHAPTER TWO

Racing Terminology

One of the difficulties for the racing enthusiast starting off with limited knowledge is to understand the various inner codes of the sport, not least the shorthand terminology. As an aid for newcomers, this is the appropriate point at which to include an A–Z glossary of some of those terms, many of which will appear later in the book.

Other racing books over the years have generally lumped all the terms into a single alphabetical list. I prefer to split them into three sections, relating (i) to the running and administration of races, (ii) betting, and (iii) the physical, stable and veterinary aspects relating to horses.

The running and administration of races

ACCEPTOR. A horse that has been entered for a specific race and which is nominated to remain in that race. This can be at various stages, especially in the case of classics.

ACEY DEUCY. The American style of riding, used because

all the American tracks are left-handed. The jockey rides with his outside leather higher than the inside to take the frequent turns. The American jockey Gary Stevens soon abandoned that style when coming to England in 1999.

ADDED MONEY. Stake money from the course, Levy Board and/or sponsors towards a race prize. A sweepstake refers to owners' entry fees.

AIDS. The equipment that controls the horse – namely, the reins, through the bit, and if necessary any blinkers, visor or hood.

ALLOWANCE. The appropriate claim allowed to apprentice (junior) riders in most races. These are 7 lb, 5 lb or 3 lb according to the number of winners ridden.

AMATEUR. An unpaid rider.

APPRENTICE. See *Allowance*. Apprentice races are restricted to these inexperienced jockeys and may be limited further to those who have ridden fewer than a given number of winners during their career.

AUTHORITY TO ACT. A registration by the racing authority (the British Horseracing Board), which enables a trainer to make entries and declarations on behalf of an owner.

BIG RACE. A feature race on a card.

BLINKERS. A hood with cap eyepieces which restrict side vision and help a horse to concentrate. Half-blinkers and visors, each offering more side visibility, are modifications.

BIT. The metal piece placed inside the horse's mouth and to which the reins are attached. The 'snaffle' is the type most commonly used, and for well-schooled horses this is normally sufficient. More severe bits with added equipment are employed for hard-pulling horses.

BREAST GIRTH (or plate). A strap to prevent the saddle slipping. Some trainers employ them regularly, but when a horse from a stable that does not do so on a regular basis is thus equipped, the chance is that the horse has a tendency to a slipping saddle, and is therefore a betting risk.

BRIDGE. The technique by which jockeys hold both reins together.

BRIDLE. The headpiece carrying the bit and the reins.

BRUSHING BOOTS. 'Boots' designed to prevent injury to a horse whose hind legs tend to brush together when galloping.

CAMERA PATROL. The official track surveillance cameras.

CANTER. The pace at which most steady conditioning work in a horse's training is conducted. Close to, you can discern a three-beat motion.

CLAIMING RACE (or claimer). A race in which horses can be entered accompanied by a price at which they can be bought, by anybody qualified (i.e. having the cash available, and not being a disqualified person). In such cases an additional fee of 15 percent must be paid to the track.

CLASS. A term indicating the category of a race, these being allotted letters from A (the highest) to H, the lowest class of race. It is also a more general measure of merit in a horse.

CLASSICS. In Britain there are five classic races, all

restricted to three-year-old entire colts and fillies. The 2000 Guineas and 1000 Guineas are both run over a mile at Newmarket in the spring. The Derby and Oaks are staged at the Epsom June meeting and are run over one and a half miles, while the St Leger, at Doncaster in September, is run over one mile, six furlongs and 132 yards. Fillies are eligible to run in all five races, but colts are excluded from the 1000 Guineas and Oaks.

CLERK OF THE COURSE. The official, licensed by the Jockey Club, who is in charge of all aspects of running a race meeting at a specific track.

CLERK OF THE SCALES. An official responsible for weighing jockeys and their equipment (including saddle) before and after races. Any unusual disparity in the two readings can bring disqualification and a fine and/or ban to any miscreant.

COLOURS. Registered colours for jacket, sleeves and cap, which are uniquely applied to each official owner. Some premier colours have been auctioned and realised large amounts, especially in the case of single colours. (I'm quite happy with my all-red jacket and red cap with white spots, thank you.)

COMING AGAIN. When a horse produces a second effort to re-pass a rival after being headed.

CONDITIONS RACE. A race in which the weights carried by certain horses will be governed by their previous achievements. Previous winners may receive penalties, while maidens or horses that have never previously run could get a weight allowance from winners.

COSH. The jockey's whip.

COUPLED. More than one horse from the same stable or

in the same ownership, which are coupled for betting purposes. This practice occurs in the USA and France, but not in Britain or Ireland.

CUP RACE. A high-class event, run over a staying distance.

DEAD-HEAT. When two or more horses are inseparable at the end of a race. Prize-money is shared. For betting purposes, your bet on either horse is settled as one half on a winner, the other half on a loser.

DECLARATIONS. Horses declared to run at the overnight stage.

DISQUALIFICATION. The demotion of a winning or other horse, because of a riding or technical infringement of the Rules of Racing.

DISTANCE. Margins between horses at the finish of a race. The term 'distance' was used historically to define a point 240 yards from the finish of races, but this physical point has become archaic. A distance is still used by the Judge to describe a superiority margin between one horse and the next finisher, which exceeds 30 lengths.

DRAW. The order in which the horses are positioned in the stalls before a Flat race.

DRIVING. The term used to describe a powerful finishing effort by a jockey.

DROPPING THE BIT. When a horse alters his momentum by releasing his pull on the bit. This can come with a wind problem, but is just as frequently a case of a horse momentarily losing concentration.

ENTIRE. A colt or full horse, that has not been gelded.

EXERCISE. The programme of work which, combined

with a comprehensive feeding regime, prepares a horse for the races and full fitness.

EXERCISE GALLOPS. A strip of ground over which fast work is conducted in preparation for racing.

FALSE-START. These tend to occur more often in jumps racing, with the double false-start and subsequent voiding of the 1993 Grand National as the most famous example. Even from stalls starts on the Flat, a false-start can be called if one or more stalls fail to open at the same time as the majority.

FILLIES. Female racehorses, aged up to and including four years. At five they become 'mares'. Horses' ages all change together on 1 January (in the Northern Hemisphere). A colt born at any time in the previous year changes from a 'foal' to a 'yearling' on 1 January.

FORFEIT. Stages in the build-up to a race. Some big races have 'entry' and 'acceptance' stages. If a horse's connections 'pay a forfeit', they are withdrawing it at the appropriate stage.

FORM. The record of previous racecourse performances of a particular horse.

FORM BOOK. A volume carrying a full record of all the races run during a season.

FORM LINE. The way in which a newspaper expresses the recent sequence of each horse's performances in a single line, with the latest position closest to (and on the left of) the horse's name.

FOUL RIDING. Deliberate breach of the Rules of Racing by a jockey. Nowadays they are categorised in decreasing levels of guilt as Dangerous, Irresponsible and Careless. The first two usually carry a riding ban and fine.

FREE RUNNER. A horse that tends to pull and fight the jockey if restraint is tried.

FRONT RUNNER. Effectively similar to a free runner, but not necessarily a hard puller, just a horse that goes best when dominating.

FURLONG. An eighth of a mile or 220 yards, translating almost exactly to 200 metres.

GALLOP. The top pace of a horse, which can be raised from a half-speed to a full gallop.

GALLOPS. The training grounds for horses.

GELDING. A castrated horse.

GIRTH. The lower band that secures the saddle on to the horse. The term also applies to a horse's width around its middle.

GOING. On the course, the state of the ground on which the horses are racing. This ranges from hard to very heavy. In Britain the intervening stages are firm, good-to-firm, good, good-to-soft and heavy.

GOT AT. Doped or (slang) nobbled.

GREEN. Inexperience in a horse on a track early in his career, characterised by not racing evenly.

HACK CANTER. A very slow canter, often by horses on their way to the start.

HALF BROTHER/SISTER. Horses from the same mother (dam) and sired by different fathers (sires).

HAND. The unit of measurement of a horse. One hand is four inches, and the height of a horse is measured at the withers, the highest point on its back. An average size for a mature horse is 16 hands, expressed as 16 hh (hands high).

HANDICAP. A race in which the weights to be carried are

framed by an official, basing those weights on the previous performances, or form, of the various horses. Those with the best form will be allotted the highest weights. For a newcomer to racing, one of the most difficult concepts to appreciate is the fact that adjustments of only a few pounds can make crucial differences in the relative performance of different horses. It is precisely the almost uncanny consistency of most horses that enables horseracing's handicap system to work so effectively.

HANDICAPPER. Official who compiles and frames handicap races.

HANDLERS. Stalls attendants whose job it is to load the runners into the stalls before the start.

HANGING. When a horse veers from a straight line. This usually suggests a problem causing pain, often in the mouth or legs.

HELD UP. A horse that is restrained (settled) behind most or all the other runners with the intention of bringing it through with a late challenge.

HOLD. A hard-pulling horse is said to take 'a strong hold'.

HORSE. In racing and breeding terms, a horse is a non-gelded mature animal of five years of age and above.

HORSEMANSHIP. Riding skill. Some jockeys are described as horsemen. In some instances this is meant as a compliment. On other occasions a rider may be a horseman but will not necessarily be a top jockey, with all the strength and finesse that implies.

HURDLES. The smaller obstacles, modelled on sheep hurdles, over which hurdle races are run. Often a jumping horse will start its career over hurdles and graduate to steeplechasing.

JUVENILE. A two-year-old.

LADS. Stable staff, male and female.

LOOKING ON. Term to describe a blatant non-trier. In these days of close scrutiny, not just by the officials but also by everyone with access to a television showing the Racing Channel, such non-triers are much more likely to be detected.

MAIDEN. In Flat racing, a horse that has not won a race. See also *Novice*.

MARTINGALE. A device to stop a horse holding its head too high. A strap under the horse's neck is joined via rings to the rein and adds extra braking potential on a headstrong animal.

MATCH. A race with only two contestants. The term 'virtual match' is used to describe a larger race in which only two of the runners have an obvious chance of winning.

MEMBERS. The principal spectator enclosure, reserved for annual members and those who pay to be members for the day.

MORNING GLORY. A horse that excels on the home gallops but is disinclined to give the expected effort when the money is at stake. (Whatever you do, never mention Killer Instinct. Who was he?)

NATIONAL HUNT (NH). The accepted term for the code of jumps racing.

NOVICE. In jumps racing, a horse that had not won a race before the current season.

NURSERY. A handicap race restricted to two-year-olds.

These races begin in midsummer, when the juveniles'
form has started to develop an established pattern.

OBJECTION. A protest about the actual running of a race.
A panel of stewards will either reject or accept a protest
by a trainer or jockey of a beaten horse. Interference
and other riding offences are the principal areas for
objection. Nowadays, investigation into the most deli-
cate incidents are usually initiated by the stewards,
leaving the actual combatants in a much less contentious situation with their colleagues and opponents.

OFF. The start of a race.

OFF/ON THE BIT. If a horse is moving happily without
needing any help from the jockey, it is 'on the bit'.
When the jockey has to urge it along, the horse is
deemed to be 'off the bit'.

ONE-PACED. A plodder.

OVER THE STICKS. A rather archaic term for jumps racing. (One summer, in the days before summer jumping, a bold blue poster was displayed outside 135 Fleet
Street. This was at the same time as the Newmarket
July meeting and said: 'Over the Sticks with the *Daily
Telegraph*'. I wonder if that marketing man is still with
us?)

OVER THE TOP. A horse that has been kept busy and is
showing the effects of his or her exertions.

PACE. The tempo at which a race is run.

PACEMAKER. The early leader. In top races a trainer may
enter a second horse to ensure that the race is run at a
suitable gallop for the stable's main hope.

PADDOCK OR PARADE RING. The area in which horses
are shown to the public before a race.

PAST THE POST (IT'S . . .) (or nailed on). Expectation of an easy victory. In racing, such expectations are liable to be disappointed.

PATTERN RACES. The top races, so-called because they are intended to be part of an overall scheme. In Britain they are divided into three groups, 1, 2 and 3. The Group 1 races, of which there are fewest, are regarded as championship races.

PECKED. When a horse stumbles and loses a damaging amount of ground as a result.

PEDIGREE. A horse's breeding.

PENALTY. Additional weight, allotted either in condition races or handicaps for wins after a certain cut-off time. Often a stable will run a horse with a penalty because of its well-being, or because its rating for future handicaps may well be raised even higher than the penalty element.

PLACING. The skill with which a trainer can maximise a horse's potential. In early 2000, Sir Mark Prescott exploited the all-weather programme to produce a sequence of seven quick wins for the filly French Spice.

PLATE. A horse's shoe.

PLATER. A horse racing at the lowest level, in selling and claiming races or 'plates'. Sometimes, a high-class plater can sweep up a surprising number of uncompetitive races in a season.

POST. 'At the post' refers to when the horses have arrived at the start. More often, though, the winning post is the object of the term.

PRESSURE. Jockeys put their mounts 'under pressure' when they ask for an additional effort.

PRICK. A minor, and sometimes not so minor, injury caused by the blacksmith when he is shoeing a horse.

PRICKER. A device at the inside of the ring through the bit, designed to prevent horses from hanging.

PULLED UP. A horse, normally in jumps racing, that has got so far behind, or is reckoned by his jockey to be lame or exhausted, is stopped to prevent unnecessary distress.

RACECARD. The day's programme sold at the track.

RACE READING. Evaluating a race, or indeed commentating on it.

RATINGS. Figures issued by the racing authorities and other independent commercial organisations. These express the merit of horses in terms of pounds. The official figures, now compiled on a central basis, are employed for providing weights to be carried in all handicap races. Where these differ from the commercial firms, the difference of opinion will generate a higher level of betting activity in some quarters.

RIG. A horse with imperfectly formed testicles. Often one may have descended and the other, usually smaller, may remain in the canal and not descend. Alternatively, he may have undergone an unsatisfactory castration operation.

RINGER. A horse whose identity has been fraudulently changed. Usually the idea is to substitute a decent performer in the guise of one markedly inferior and land a gamble.

DEAD RINGER A replica of someone else, in horses or people.

ROARER. A horse who has gone in its wind. When he exercises, he makes a noise, a serious defect.

ROGUE'S BADGE. The old name for blinkers, which still tend to be used most on unwilling horses, or rogues.

RUNNING ON. Staying on strongly at the finish of a race, without actually winning.

SALES. Auctions where horses change hands. Commercial and private breeders offer horses at various sales through the year. The most expensive are the leading yearling sales in Kentucky (Keeneland), Newmarket (Tattersalls), and Ireland (Goffs). Horses can realise millions of dollars or pounds at these sales.

SCOPE. Physical potential in a horse, who is often the unfinished article.

SCRATCHING. Withdrawal of a horse from a race into which it had been an original entry.

SELLER. Race where the winner is offered for sale by auction. In Britain, after such events, all the other contestants are available to be claimed too.

SHADOW BAND OR ROLL. Sheepskin noseband, designed to keep a horse's head low. See also *Martingale*.

SHORT RUNNER (or non-stayer). A horse that cannot give optimum effort for the full distance of a race.

SITTING AGAINST. Restraining a horse.

SNAFFLE. The normal racing bit, attached to a single rein.

SPREAD PLATE. A shoe that has come off on the way to the start, or during a race.

STEEPLECHASE. A race run over fences.

STEWARDS. Racing officials who adjudicate on disputes.

STIPES. Paid officials (stipendiary stewards) whose role it is to direct the other amateur stewards through any contentious issues on a race day.

STRIDING OUT. A horse showing a good stride on its way to the start.

STRING. The full complement of a training stable.

STUD FARM. A breeding establishment.

STUD BOOK. The official record of the pedigrees of all thoroughbred racehorses.

SURCINGLE. An extra girth which goes over the saddle.

TAKING MY GROUND. The basis of an objection by a jockey who believes an opponent has crossed over and caused him or her to lose a place or more in the process.

TATTERSALLS. Britain's leading bloodstock auctioneers, based in Newmarket. The name has also come to describe the second stand, next to the Members, on British courses.

TIGHT REIN. Used when a horse is apparently travelling well through its race, with the rider having his or her 'hands full'.

TONGUE TIE. A means to ensure that a horse will not 'swallow its tongue' and thereby lose the capacity to take in air. In 1999, the rules were changed so that the application of tongue ties has to be declared along with the overnight declaration to run.

TOUT. Work watcher – sadly, a dying breed.

TRAINED ON. A horse that has continued to improve as it matured.

TRIAL GALLOPS. A serious workout, usually designed to test a horse's readiness for a major race. Most trainers in the modern era rarely ask their horses to undergo such extreme tests, reserving the main exertion for the track where there is money and glory to be won.

UNDER ORDERS. The horses are set to start the race. Any horse withdrawn after this point will be deemed to have been a participant for betting purposes.

UNSADDLING ENCLOSURE. Enclosure where the first four horses return to unsaddle prior to their jockeys' weighing in.

WALKOVER. A 'race' with a single, unopposed runner. In some countries horses are required to complete the full distance to win a walkover, whereas in Britain they only have to go a short way down the track and canter past the winning post to earn their prize.

WARNING-OFF. A disqualification. The result is that the disqualified person cannot appear at licensed racing premises, including racecourses and racing stables.

WEIGHING-OUT. Before each race, all jockeys are weighed with their equipment (including the saddle containing varying lead weights) to confirm that the correct weight will be carried. See also *Weighing-in*.

WEIGHING-IN. After a race the jockeys must return to the Clerk of the Scales to be reweighed. Often, only the first four jockeys in a race are required to weigh-in.

WEIGHING ROOM. The jockeys' private changing room. The scales are actually situated outside the weighing room, in front of the Clerk of the Scales.

WEIGHT-FOR-AGE. A sliding scale of relative weights that becomes automatically adjusted according to age of horse and race distances throughout the passage of the year. By the end of a racing season, these differences are reduced.

WORK. The combination of an exercise programme, in conjunction with skilful and balanced feeding, will produce a horse fit enough to run a good race.

WORKMANLIKE. An accepted term for a strong, sound animal who looks the type to win races or, alternatively, in performance terms a run that was adequate but unremarkable.

Betting terms

ACCUMULATOR. A bet in which four or more horses are backed in a single wager. The money accumulates quickly, with the original stake and all the winnings passing from horse to horse.

BALANCING A BOOK. How a bookmaker spreads the risk, by running a field book and evaluating the individual losing and winning horses in the book. He will hedge with other bookies to bring the book into a workable balanced position.

BAR. The lowest odds available about horses not actually named in the list of prices. A call of 'eight-to-one bar one' by a bookmaker would mean that in this race, every horse, apart from the favourite, is available at 8-1 or higher.

BEES (or beeswax). Cockney rhyming slang for betting tax. Other terms in this vein include Burlington (Bertie) for 100-30 and cockle (short for Cock and Hen) for 10-1 or £10.

BETTING FORECAST. The predicted odds in the morning newspapers on the races to be run that day.

BETTING STABLE. One in which the trainer and owners are known or suspected to be serious backers who aim to land gambles through the season.

BETTING WITHOUT THE FAVOURITE. If the favourite is at very short odds, some bookmakers will prefer to ignore him for betting purposes, framing a separate market on the remaining runners.

BOGEY. The biggest loser in a bookmaker's book on a certain race.

BUYING MONEY. The practice of backing short-priced horses. When a horse is available at odds-on, it takes more money as a stake to produce a smaller winning amount.

CANADIAN. A bet involving five selections. This is a full-cover bet, comprising ten doubles, ten trebles, five four-horse accumulators and one five-horse accumulator. That totals 26 bets.

CARPET. The betting-ring term for a horse priced at 3-1. Hence 'double carpet' for 33-1, a price much beloved by journalist John McCririck.

CENTURY. £100.

COMMISSION. A bet placed on behalf of a stable. Where the stable is renowned as a betting one, this commission is likely to cause the odds to contract.

COMPUTER STRAIGHT FORECAST (CSF). The bookmakers' version of a Tote Exacta. The punter has to nominate the first two horses in a race in the correct order (or in either order for a 'reverse forecast' with double the stake).

COUP. A heavy gamble, based on skilful placing of a horse, often in easier company, following some poor races in better class.

DOUBLE. A bet on two horses, whereby any return from the first horse passes on to the second.

DRIFTER. A horse whose odds drift out (lengthen). This can be because the racecourse intelligence system has heard it is unfancied, or it can simply look out of fettle. (The course pundit John McCririck latches on to drifters in his role as Channel Four's betting analyst. He will shout: 'This one cannot possibly win' – and while he does get it wrong sometimes, the inescapable fact is that horses drift in the market usually for a good reason and do not win.)

EACH WAY. Effectively two bets, one for a win and one for a placing.

EVEN MONEY (or evens). A bet at 'even money' produces a profit equal to the stake, where there is no tax element (as on the racecourse).

EXACTA. A Tote bet, wherein the first two horses home must be named in the correct order. The former Dual Forecast bet on the Tote was withdrawn in January 2000. In that, two horses were again selected and the order between the pair, as long as they were first and second, did not matter.

FACES. Punters who are considered shrewd or are well known within the betting ring. (A 'face' can expect to be greeted with 'What have you come here for on a Monday in January?')

FALSE PRICE. Short odds that do not truly reflect a horse's chances, perhaps because of the reputation of the stable or jockey, or because the bookmakers want to pursuade punters to back other horses instead.

FAVOURITE. The shortest-priced horse in a race.

FLIMPING. Paying out (by bookmakers) under the true odds.

GOLIATH. As the name implies, this is a bet of massive proportions, involving eight horses. A full-cover bet encompasses 28 doubles, 56 trebles, 70 four-horse accumulators, 56 five-horse accumulators, 28 six-horse accumulators, 8 seven-horse accumulators and a final eight-horse accumulator, for 247 bets in total. If they all win, book your world cruise.

GRAND. £1000

HEDGING. The means by which bookmakers with bigger liabilities than they would prefer on certain horses can trade with other bookies to redress their position.

HEINZ. A multiple bet involving six horses. These are backed in 15 doubles, 20 trebles, 15 four-horse accumulators, 6 five-horse accumulators and a six-horse accumulator, to provide 57 varieties of bet – hence Heinz.

INFORMATION. Inside intelligence, often from a stable, which reveals that the horse is fancied to win (or not).

JACKPOT. A Tote bet where all six winners of the first six races on a nominated card must be found. This bet no longer operates on Saturdays (see *Tote Scoop6*). Any unwon money is carried forward. During big meetings, pools will grow and can generate massive payouts.

JOLLY. The favourite in a race.

JOINT FAVOURITES (JF). Two horses start at the same

odds, but are shorter than the rest of the field. 'Co-favourites' (CF) is the term describing three or more horses sharing the head of the market.

KITE. Slang for a cheque.

KNOCK. Owing or non-payment, usually punter against bookmaker but very occasionally the other way around.

MARKET. The overall betting arena on any race. In the spectator enclosures, the pressure of bets on one horse rather than another, and the need for bookmakers to secure their position and avoid unnecessary risks, determines the eventual make-up of the market in terms of individual odds (prices).

MARKET MOVER. A horse that shortens abruptly in the betting (the opposite of drifting).

MONKEY. Slang for £500.

NAP. A racing tipster's best bet of the day. There may also be a next-best (nb). The major national newspaper tipsters, and many from the provinces, compete for the Coral/*Racing Post* naps table. There are two competitions, one in the summer exactly spanning the turf Flat season, and another in the winter. (Before its closure, the *Sporting Life* ran the table with Corals and I was lucky enough to win it three times.)

NOT OFF. A horse reckoned a non-trier in the betting ring.

OVER-BROKE. A betting book with no profit margin.

OVER-ROUND. Betting with the margin in the book-maker's favour.

PATENT. A bet involving three horses in three singles, three doubles and a treble, making seven bets in all.

PLACE ONLY. A Tote bet in which a punter selects a horse to finish in the frame ('placed'). For betting purposes, where there are fewer than four runners, only winners qualify as placed horses. With between five and seven runners, two places are paid. When there are eight or more runners in any field, three places are paid, except for handicaps containing 16 or more runners, when a fourth place is added. Bookmakers offer place-only bets only in exceptional circumstances.

PLACEPOT. The Tote's flagship bet requiring the punter to select a horse to finish in the frame (see *Place only*) in each of the first six races on a card.

PONY. Slang for £25.

PRICE. The odds available about a particular horse.

PUNTER. In racing, specifically someone who bets.

QUADPOT. A mini-Placepot on the last four legs of that Placepot.

RAG. An unfancied horse ('complete outsider') in the betting market.

RAILS. The line of bookmakers between the Members and Tattersalls spectator enclosures. Odds are called and punters can bet with these bookmakers in cash, on credit or with debit cards.

RULE 4. The shortened name for Tattersalls' Rule 4. This rule deals with the situation when a horse is withdrawn from a race, perhaps through lameness or because the ground is not considered suitable for it, after the bookmakers have advertised their prices. Depending on that horse's price at the time of withdrawal, deductions will be made from winning bets struck earlier at a fixed price. When it is too late to form a new market, deductions will be made from all bets. The deduction from winnings is on a sliding scale, from 5p in the £ if a horse was between 10-1 and 14-1, up to 75p in the £ for a horse withdrawn at odds shorter than 30-100.

SCORE. Slang for £20.

SILVER RING. The cheapest spectator enclosure.

SKINNER. An unbacked winning horse in a book, which means the bookmaker keeps all the money bet on the race.

SPRINGER (or steamer). A horse that suddenly springs into notice in the market. Often the betting momentum continues, the horse continuing to shorten as bookies' liabilities increase, right up to the off.

STARTING PRICES (SPs). The prices available at the 'off' for all the horses in a race. These are used to settle all off-course bets where the punter has not otherwise the option of 'taking a price' when placing the bet.

SUPER-HEINZ. A seven-horse bet, consisting of 21 doubles, 35 trebles, 35 four-horse accumulators, 21 five-horse accumulators, 7 six-horse accumulators, and a seven-horse accumulator, to provide a total of 120 bets.

TIC-TAC. Bookmakers' employees (spot them on their raised boxes near the rails bookmakers) who use a hand signalling system whereby prices on offer and amounts of money being wagered can be represented. Their task is to ensure that the various bookmakers employing them can stay ahead of the betting trends around the enclosures. Some accepted slang names for prices relate to the position of the signals in tic-tac. Thus ear'ole is 6-4, face means 5-2, and hand 5-1.

TISSUE. A list of prices, available to course bookmakers, predicting the likely opening prices for each race when betting begins.

TOTE. The organisation which has a monopoly on pool betting in Britain. The Tote's full name is the Horserace Totalisator Board.

TOTE DIRECT. An organisation which links the Tote with bookmakers who offer Tote odds bets, placed into pools via machines on shop counters. Coral were original partners, joined later by Ladbrokes. As of spring 2000, William Hill had elected to remain outside Tote Direct.

TOTE SCOOP6. A bet launched in 1999. The punter's money is split between a win pool (25 percent), place pool (25 percent) and bonus pool (20 percent), the remaining 30 percent being split between the Tote and its Tote Direct partners. It is based on six televised races, currently on Channel Four. The bonus pool is available only after the win pool has been won on the previous weekend.

TRICAST. An extension of the *computer straight forecast*. Here, the punter has to select the first three horses in the correct order. Dividends can be high if outsiders dominate the result in big handicap races.

TRIFECTA. The Tote's version of the tricast. Unlike that bet, which often goes unwon (luckily for bookmakers), any unwon Trifecta pools are directed to future races, normally on the following day.

TRIXIE. The most simple multiple bet involving three horses. These are backed in three doubles and a treble to make four bets in total.

YANKEE. Still one of the most popular betting shop wagers. Four horses are combined for six doubles, four trebles and an accumulator for a total of 11 bets. In many cases, though, it has been eclipsed by the Lucky Fifteen. This bet is basically a yankee, but with four singles applied to the horses. To make this bet more attractive, the bookmakers have offered double the odds in the event of a single winner. Therefore, such a bet with three losers and an 8-1 winner (paid as a 16-1 winner) will show a small profit. The punter who stays loyal to the yankee will be 11 points behind on the same four horses.

In the stable

ACTION. How the horse moves. A so-called 'daisy-cutting' action where the horse covers the ground with ease suggests a fast-ground performer. A horse exhibiting a high knee action will probably prefer softer ground, as on firm going it will hit the ground hard and put pressure on knee and ankle joints.

ADRENALIN. A hormone naturally secreted from the body glands to aid muscle action. Generally when a horse is hit by the whip, adrenalin flow is increased.

AMISS. The term relating to racing fillies or broodmares when they are in season. This often affects adversely performances by fillies.

ANAEMIA. A blood deficiency. This is often the cause of loss of weight and reduced strength.

BACK AT THE KNEE. A conformation defect. From the

side, the knees curve backwards and this often increases the risk of unsoundness.

BARREL. The body portion of the horse, between the front and hind legs.

BARREN. A mare that has not become pregnant after being covered by a stallion, sometimes more than one.

BAY. The colour of a horse between dark and light brown. This type has a dark mane and tail and generally with black on the legs.

BIG. A paddock term, designating a horse carrying excess flesh, and therefore one that is unlikely to be fully fit. Some horses can run well, however, when appearing 'big'.

BLEEDER. A horse with a tendency to break blood-vessels.

BLISTER. An irritant, applied to the legs of a horse with a sprain. It causes inflammation aimed at quickening the normal healing process.

BLOODSTOCK. Accepted generic term for thoroughbred horses.

BLOW UP. A horse is said to blow up when, often in its first race or coming back after a long layoff, it suddenly stops when the flow of air gives out.

BOG SPAVIN. Swelling on the front inside of a hock. Rest needed.

BONE. A term describing the thickness of bone on a horse's legs. Measurement is taken around the cannon bone, below the knee.

BOX (or loose box). A horse's living quarters.

BREAKING. The initial process when a horse enters training. At first it will be taught to circle in both directions on a lunge rope. Then in time, after it has accepted having a bit and reins attached to the mouth, it will be 'driven' with long reins and eventually 'backed' and finally 'ridden away'.

BRISKET. Lowest part of the chest.

BROOM MARE (DAM). Mare used for breeding.

BROWN. True chocolate colour, with black legs, mane and tail.

BUTE (BUTAZOLIDIN). A drug used on horses with muscular problems. It is permitted for use in conjunction with a race in most US states, but not in Britain, where discovery in a horse's system after a post-race test will bring disqualification and a sanction on the trainer.

CANNON BONE. The bone under the knee. Where the bone is thin, the horse is likely to have problems of unsoundness.

CAST. A horse is cast when it lies down in its box and gets into a position, often in the corner, from which it cannot stand up. Injuries often occur from the resulting panic.

CHESTNUT. Colour from yellow to gold, or a liver colour, together with mane and tail of a lighter colour. The bright (or 'flashy') chestnut with four white socks is often a horse that superstitious, and some not so superstitious, racing people steer away from. At the same time, there are many instances of champions of just that description. Arthur Stephenson, the renowned trainer, used to say: 'I've never known a good horse be a bad colour.'

CHESTNUTS. Horny growths (callosities) on the inside of a horses' legs, either above the knee or below the hock.

COLIC. Severe pain in a horse's belly caused by spasm or twisting of the gut. This can be of varying intensity and sometimes, if not spotted in time, can result in death.

CONFORMATION. The make and shape of a horse.

CREST. The upper line of a horse's neck.

CURB. A strain, revealed when the tendon thickens at the back of the hock.

CUT. Another term for gelding.

DOCK. The upper, solid part of the tail.

ELBOW. The upper joint of the foreleg.

FEED. Horses in full training consume very large amounts of food. Oats, bulk feeds and supplements, with added extras immediately before a race, are the normal diet and even this is liable to be increased as the fitness regime develops.

FETLOCK. The joint at the bottom of the cannon bone, connecting to the pastern.

FILLING. When a leg swells for one of many reasons.

FIRING. A more severe remedy than *blistering*, aimed at hastening recovery from leg injuries. Hot iron (line firing) or deep penetration (pin firing) have become unfashionable, as it is accepted that rest is the only proper cure.

FOREARM. The upper part of the foreleg.

FROG. The part of the sole of a horse's foot which helps grip the ground when galloping.

GOOD-TOPPED. A good back line, together with a well-shaped body and barrel.

HOBDAYING. A surgical operation on the larynx designed to improve flow of air into the lungs. It often has an unsatisfactory result.

HOCK. The joint on the hind leg, at the top of the cannon bone.

JOINTS. Knee, fetlock (or ankle) and hock, all areas of potential problems.

LIGHT. When a horse runs up light, it cannot take the programme of training and racing without losing condition.

LIGHT OF BONE. Too narrow around the cannon bone.

LONG IN THE BACK. A horse with a long thin back, and therefore one which could develop weakness. Rangy horses can also have a long back, but with sufficient substance and width to compensate.

MAKING A NOISE. Unsound in wind (breathing).

MUSCLED UP. Obvious signs of muscle development, often accompanied by an excellent, bright coat.

NEARSIDE. The horse's left side, the side on which it is led.

OATS. The main feed for racehorses. Many stables in the modern era have switched to proprietary 'nuts' or 'cake' as the main feed. The Godolphin operation has its own custom-made feed mill, and all the feed for Godolphin horses is shipped from Dubai to the various training centres.

OFFSIDE. The right-hand side of the horse.

OVER AT THE KNEE. As it sounds, the knees develop forward of the main part of the leg. This is not normally regarded as potentially harmful for training purposes, but purists will take exception, especially at the sales.

PASTERN. The sloping bone above the foot.

QUARTERS. The horse's rear end.

SESAMOID. Two small bones within the fetlock joint, frequently an area of potential problems. Sesamoids can crack or break.

SORE SHINS. A regular problem with two-year-olds when they begin training. When a young horse gets sore shins, it is telling the trainer to ease up on its work.

SICKLE HOCKS. Over-bent hocks.

SOUNDNESS. A sound horse is one with no physical problems. In most transactions between buyer and seller, a soundness warranty is required. If a horse fails a veterinary inspection, it is deemed to be unsound for whatever specific defect is found and the buyer need proceed no further with the deal.

STIFLE. The upper joint on a hind leg.

STRANGLES. A contagious disease of the nose and throat which entails a lengthy rest period before training can recommence.

TENDONS. The sinews connecting the muscles to the bones of the leg. A strained tendon is known as a 'bowed tendon', because it springs outwards like a bow and is easily identified. Horses with badly bowed tendons are often unsuitable for racing even after long rest periods.

WITHERS. The connecting point between the backbone and the neck.

CHAPTER THREE

The World of Betting

Introduction

It would be hard to exaggerate the need for a strong betting market to maintain the credibility of the British racing industry.

In the late 1990s racing faced a number of major challenges, especially from the National Lottery which began in 1995. The latter's initial impact on racing became slightly less marked towards the end of the decade, but by then the ever-resourceful major off-course combines had been keen to exploit its attraction for their own purposes. Thus they hatched their own imitation lottery, called the '49s' bet, based in the same way on selecting ball numbers. Unlike the National Lottery, which is restricted to two draws per week, 49s initially were drawn on a once-a-day basis. This soon became twice a day, morning and afternoon, with an extra third draw on days when night racing is broadcast from the shops.

A second major threat to racing's share of the betting-shop 'cake' is the burgeoning betting on other sports, especially Premier League soccer, cricket and golf. It is easy to understand the bookmakers' preference for these other activities, and especially the advent of the AWP ('amusements with prizes') machines that are a feature of the modern shop. It is simply a matter of profitability. In betting shops, the AWP machines cost virtually nothing to maintain and there is absolutely no chance of their providing anything other than a solid, regular profit.

Other sports betting is profitable. For instance, betting on single soccer matches – allowed when there is live Sky or other TV coverage – offers three possible results, home win, away win or draw. The bookmakers' margin is a controlled 12 percent on average and taken throughout the country; again it is almost impossible for them to lose over a period.

Greyhound racing attracts the second highest level of betting after horseracing. Bookmakers have found that the 'ideal' formula for a day's programming is three afternoon horserace meetings timed ten minutes apart, with a couple of 12- or 14-race greyhound meetings to split the remaining spare air time. These dog races are staggered at around 20 minutes at each of the tracks, which enables one dog race to be run between any two horseraces.

A number of the tracks selected to provide the greyhound service are owned by either Ladbrokes or Coral, two of the 'Big Three' (the other being William Hill). It is hard to escape the view that the betting markets at Ladbrokes' Crayford and Monmore Green, and Coral's Hove and Romford, are compliant with the track owners' requirements. Betting margins are greatly in favour of the bookmakers – hardly surprisingly as very few racegoers bother to attend these meetings. It is as if the result does not matter.

Much of greyhound betting is in fact based on forecasts, which involves placing the first two out of six in the correct order. The effect of poor individual prices about six greyhounds is to make the forecast dividends even more markedly depressed, as they are calculated from a starting-price based formula.

We will be looking elsewhere at the Levy Board and its handling of racing finances. In this context, it is suffi-cient to explain that money currently goes into the horseracing industry by virtue of a deduction from horserace bets placed off-course, which can be paid in two ways by the punter. Remember – and this is something bookmakers often forget when they claim to be paying it – that the money that goes back to racing is paid exclusively by the punter.

For each £100 wagered off-course, £9 is deducted by the bookmaker. This can be either as a supplement to the stake paid by the punter at the time the bet is placed, or as a deduction (obviously a bigger amount) from winning wagers. The 9 percent deduction encompasses the rate of General Betting Duty (6.75 percent) to go to the government, and an element of 1.49 percent of turnover to go to the Levy. The latter pays for much of the funding of racing, and in the year 2000 it was expected to amount to £69 million.

It is easy to see that there is an unused margin – around 0.75 percent – from the bookmakers' 9 percent 'tax' deduction. Bookmakers unashamedly retain it, explaining it away in various ways. In regard to betting on other sports and greyhound racing, however, there is no payment to be paid to the Levy and the bookmakers' profitability is again higher

Even with horse bets, a big losing wager for the book-maker can have its compensations. A £100 winning bet on a 10-1 chance provides a windfall consolation if the tax element has not been paid by the punter at the time of striking the bet. A return, including the original stake, of £1100 generates £99 in 'tax' deduction at 9 percent, so the actual net return to the punter is £1001. Hence the bookmaker loses just £901 to the punter. This means that the bookmaker's liability lessens by £90 compared with his loss of £991 (£1000 minus £9) if tax is paid at point of sale.

Making a book

The supply end of the betting-shop bookmakers' business is the racetrack. In a way the bookmaker is a hostage to the betting ring, but, naturally, the professionals in the ring are aware that they need to be as prudent as they can, without causing punters to withdraw their patronage.

Bookmaking is based on a balancing act. All odds can be expressed as a percentage figure by doing a simple calculation. Consider the price of 10-1. Express that as 10, then add 1 to make 11. Take the reciprocal of 11 – i.e. one-eleventh – and then convert that to a percentage; that is about 9 percent. The percentages corresponding to the traditional odds are calculated for you in the box opposite.

ODDS AS PERCENTAGES

Odds on		Evens		Odds against
1-100	99	50	100-1	1
1-66	98.5		66-1	1.5
1-50	98		50-1	2
1-33	97		33-1	3
1-25	96		25-1	4
1-20	95		20-1	5
1-16	94		16-1	6
1-14	93		14-1	7
1-12	92		12-1	8
1-11	91		11-1	8
1-10	90		10-1	9
1-9	90		9-1	10
1-8	89		8-1	11
2-15	88		15-2	12
1-7	87.5		7-1	12.5
2-13	86		13-2	13
1-6	86		6-1	14
2-11	85		11-2	15
1-5	84		5-1	16
2-9	81		9-2	18
1-4	80		4-1	20
2-7	78		7-2	22
3-10	77		10-3	23
1-3	75		3-1	25
4-11	73		11-4	27
2-5	71		5-2	28
4-9	69		9-4	31
1-2	67		2-1	33
8-15	65		15-8	35
4-7	64		7-4	36
8-13	62		13-8	38
4-6	60		6-4	40
8-11	58		11-8	42
4-5	56		5-4	44
10-11	53		11-10	47

Odds are framed around the basis of £100, so in a book a 10-1 chance would take out £100 to the nearest pound with a £9 bet. The actual take out is only £99, which margin of error would be just in the bookmaker's favour.

It is easy to see, from the above step-by-step calculation, that an even-money chance represents 50 percent. Evens equal 1-1. Express that as 1 and add 1, makes 2. The reciprocal is one-half, or 50 percent, and 50 percentage points in the book.

Where a horse is at odds-on, it represents more than 50 percent. Heavy backing of an odds-on chance makes that horse even closer to the hundred points' margin, but the snag for the bookmaker is that such horses, especially when there is plenty of punter confidence behind them in the ring, are very likely winners. Outsiders reflect much smaller numbers – for example a 20-1 shot is five percentage points, a 50-1 chance is two points and a 100-1 chance only one point. For practical purposes, course bookmakers disregard such outsiders as in practice they are very rarely found in the average book.

In a competitive market, the odds usually start more strongly in favour of the bookmaker. In the south at the top meetings, and at tracks like York, Doncaster, Chester, Aintree and Haydock in the north, bookmakers will tend to extend the odds on certain horses to attract backers. All the time, they will attempt, by skilful manipulation of the odds on their boards to keep to a minimum the losers in the book. Some bookmakers are particular students of the sport and will have an opinion of the concept of 'value'. They will be more prepared to take large bets against certain short-priced horses and will slant their overall book accordingly.

A visitor to the betting ring nowadays will still see the same division between rails and Tattersalls bookmakers. The rails operators quite literally stand immediately behind the dividing partition between the Members and Tattersalls enclosures. Punters can bet with the rails bookmakers from the Members side of the course, but would need to go through to Tattersalls for a boards bet. There has been a concerted campaign among rails bookmakers for changes to be made so that they can display odds on boards in the way their counterparts traditionally have in 'Tatts'.

There is no such disparity between the two groups of bookmakers in Ireland; but the recent series of sales of seniority positions or the old-type 'pitches', where generally rails positions were far less valuable than Tatts places, was staged on the understanding that the status quo would be maintained.

Should the rails situation change, then clearly those positions immediately next to the Members enclosure, with its preponderance of more wealthy racegoers, would become far more valuable – a prospect not lost on those bookmakers who have paid large 'transfer fees'.

Course bookmakers are increasingly adopting technology to do much of the mathematical work that was hitherto undertaken by their quick-witted clerks. They used a large ledger in which all bets were recorded, keeping a running tally of the liability on each horse in the race, and a master figure of the total field money in that race. The quickest clerks could advise the boss that one horse or another was 'out of step' with the rest of the book, and skilful 'hedging' – the process by which a bookmaker lays off or shares the liability with a colleague – could put the book back into balance.

Now, instead of handing out thick card tickets, from March 2000 bookmakers have used new computers that issue small, flimsy tickets, calculate liability and, above all, eliminate the often tried, but far less frequently achieved, attempt to claim a winning bet from a losing ticket. The new-style ticket shows the horse's number, the odds at which the bet was placed, and the total pay-out in the event of that horse's winning.

Most of the changes have been accompanied by at best scepticism by the old guard, and at worst a feeling that the betting ring is dying and will soon be moribund. The new blood has altered the balance, especially for the punter, with margins down and a product that has little in common with that presented only a few years ago.

Betting with the Tote

Since its formation under an Act of Parliament in 1928, the Horserace Totalisator Board has held the sole franchise on pool betting on all horseracing in Britain. It accepted its first bets in August of the following year at Carlisle and Newmarket, and has provided the model for pool betting in many other countries. While most racing countries have eliminated bookmakers totally – and have therefore enjoyed the benefits of monopoly in their pool betting – Britain's Tote has languished in comparison as a poor relation.

For most racing fans the image of the Tote is a distinct one. Older racegoers will remember the former tickets, which were torn manually from a book, but one's contact with the Tote on racecourses is now usually with a female operator in a bright red uniform. The transactions were formerly slow and deliberate; now the issuing of tickets is usually rapid, and the dividends are declared promptly in most cases. That is not to say that the system is foolproof – it has been known for a potentially winning ticket to be issued incorrectly, resulting in irritation for the punter. The latest machines have yet to be perfected.

Britain's on-course Tote has suffered because of the way in which so much of the betting in this country goes off-course. Betting shops, even those owned by the Tote's off-course cash arm, Tote Bookmakers, operate on the basis of fluctuating prices in the run up to each race, and starting prices at the 'off' – in each case reflecting odds available at the track. Because of this, the on-course Tote pool does not truly reflect the actual volume of betting on races, especially at the smaller tracks. However, the development of the Tote Direct alliance between the Tote and co-founder Coral, with the later addition of Ladbrokes as a third partner, has had the effect of enlarging some pools. Win and place ('each way') betting has never thrived even under Tote Direct; but other bets, especially the Placepot which has become the organisation's biggest and most consistent success story, offer promise of greater achievements in the future.

Tote Direct

The big bookmaking firms were always suspicious of the Tote, so it was a great surprise when the alliance between the Tote and the Coral group, then owned by Bass, spawned Tote Direct. Under this alliance, terminals were installed in betting shops, and initially Jackpot and Placepot bets were accepted into the major pools. Hitherto these had been fuelled only by cash on the specific course, added to bets from the Tote's own credit customers.

Later, course-to-course betting was introduced as the technology improved, allowing on-course punters to bet at the Tote windows on the 'away' races. Before the advent of Tote Direct, Placepot pools in midweek could total as little as £3000. In contrast, during the winter of 2000, even the weakest midweek programme would normally attract around £30,000 into the Placepot pools, which swell to £50,000 or more at the big weekend meetings.

So, Coral's partnership, boosted later in the 1990s by Ladbrokes, had a beneficial effect, but this was hardly surprising. From a deduction approaching 30 percent in most pools, the participating bookmakers receive a commission of more than 20 percent. This level of incentive will need to be reduced in the middle and long term so that payout dividends to punters will be competitive compared with starting price bets.

The Tote's long period (1971–97) under the chairmanship of Woodrow, later Lord, Wyatt is generally regarded as one of opportunities lost. Lord Wyatt's instinctive understanding of the political world enabled him to persuade successive Prime Ministers and Home Secretaries that he should remain in his post long after his effective prime. The succession of Peter Jones, in August 1997, has brought much-needed change and above all flexibility. Jones, who made his name with the Omnicom advertising agency, has been manifest in his vigorous reappraisal of the products available to Tote punters.

The Jackpot bet

Throughout its long lifetime the Tote Jackpot has had a chequered existence. The problem has always been to entice enough punters in the early stages of a build-up to a big pool. In weeks when there might be an original guarantee of just £10,000 at the start of a Jackpot's lifetime, the small pools on offer for the task of picking all the winners on a six-race card give little incentive for the betting shop punter to risk much more than a minimal amount. Why be the cannon-fodder for the big players to gain the spoils later, when the levels are more enticing to the syndicates.

The Jackpot's problem nowadays is that, since it is confined to weekday meetings, it grows far too slowly. Until the Cheltenham festival or Royal Ascot there is little chance of a huge build-up to excite the punters. It is no wonder that the Fakenham fixture on the Friday in March after the conclusion of Cheltenham's big meeting can become the centre of the racing universe, in domestic betting terms at least. Massive pools can be carried forward to the West Norfolk track. Then you see the money roll in and, pleasure of pleasures, often a small punter with a single £1 stake gets into the big-money scene.

In 1999, I thought it would be nice to revisit Fakenham,

a track I had not seen for more than 30 years. Then I was a very green member of the racing desk of the Press Association and, in the full flush of youth, walked the course – it is only seven furlongs round. My colleague was David Thomas, son of the late Len Thomas, one of the doyens for many years of the now sadly defunct *Sporting Life* newspaper. David and I found the gradients of the sharp, intimate country track more testing than expected, and on this return visit I felt no inclination to test the now badly broken wind in similar fashion.

The reason for the return trip was the fact that £295,473 was carried forward from the Gold Cup card at Cheltenham. This was courtesy of the losing bets of the legion of Irishmen whose bankers all bit the dust – Le Coudray (in the Stayers Hurdle), Florida Pearl (in the Gold Cup) and Elegant Lord (in the Foxhunters).

At Fakenham, manageable fields with eight, eight, nine and nine again in the first four races gave the bet a winnable aspect. Those like me who placed a small, low-stake permutation bet were therefore disappointed when all four favourites obliged, at 2-1, 2-1, 11-10 and 10-11. With two more hot favourites to follow in a hunter chase and a maiden hurdle, the prospect was of thousands of winners and an embarrassing outcome for all, after the customary hype from television, newspapers and the Tote itself.

Fortunately for the Tote and a few lucky syndicate members, those who preferred the successful Tommy's Webb, an outsider, rather than the odds-on Mr Dick in the hunter chase reduced the remaining tickets to barely a handful (just short of 25). That left an 11-runner novice hurdle, which looked as near a two-horse race as could be possible beforehand.

Two and a bit circuits of Fakenham make up two miles, and that was the reason for what can only be described as a chapter of misfortune. On the first circuit, one of the hurdles was badly damaged as the field negotiated it. Next time round, the entire field, with the exception of third favourite Jamorin Dancer, bypassed the hurdle on the wrong side. Jamorin Dancer, uniquely, actually jumped the flight. When his rider realised what had happened, he returned to the hurdle, bypassing it on the correct side, the outside. All the field, without Jamorin Dancer, were adjudged to have transgressed the relevant Rule of Racing and were disqualified. At this point the judge, Dave Smith, left his box, believing Jamorin Dancer had pulled up. He was therefore not in position when Jamorin Dancer quite correctly passed the winning line. For the record, Hurricane Jane, the odds-on favourite, came over the line nine lengths clear of Tangshan.

The Jackpot was therefore not decided in favour of Jamorin Dancer. All 24.69 tickets on that leg were treated as winners, each receiving £19,638. Few of the winners were too upset as the bulk of tickets had been on Hurricane Jane.

One footnote is that even with four outright favourite winners and a void final leg, the Placepot (picking placed horses) on that day paid an amazing £594. The Quadpot, another much maligned Tote bet which is a four-race 'Placepot' based on the last four legs of its big brother, paid £239 to a £1 stake. That was entirely due to the unlikely result of the hunter chase in which Tommy's Webb, the 20-1 chance, was followed home by Chester Ben (33-1) and A Right Set To (20-1).

With all respect to Fakenham, over the years it has rarely been the centre of attraction. A mixture of luck, garnished with a tiny modicum of prescience, took me to the middle of nowhere and produced a good on-the-spot yarn for readers of the *Daily Telegraph*. In 2000, Fakenham was again the beneficiary of a big carryover from Cheltenham. In this case a carry forward of £278,182 from a part-won pool at the last day at the festival spiralled to just over £800,000. New money exceeding £500,000 – the sixth highest amount bet into a Jackpot in a single day – showed the bet's continued value, in the right circumstances. Certainly, the 26.54 winning tickets, collecting £21,438 for a £1 investment, represents continued evidence of the interest in racing on a wider scale. On a daily basis, though, the Jackpot has been supplanted in the public perception by the success of the Tote Scoop6. Therefore, it is probably time to give it a rethink, in the way that the Trifecta and Quadpot clearly need adjustments.

In the old days the bet could be won if a punter selected the first five winners. Anything to make it more winnable would be appreciated by punters – placepots are currently more attractive. Perhaps restricting the starting points of the Jackpots to the racing festivals is the answer. At such meetings the Tote does not mind offering a big initial guarantee for the first-day pool, and punters act accordingly.

Even so, in 1999 the Jackpot at Cheltenham grew

steadily in the face of much stronger activity on the Placepot. On the opening day at Cheltenham when Istabraq won his second Champion Hurdle, there was £77,281 carried forward to the meeting from an unwon Jackpot. Compare that with the £3020 dividend for the Placepot, simply to find six placed horses. With the latter, 117 tickets correctly predicted one of the possible 1728 ways of having a scoring line. That first-day Cheltenham card comprised three non-handicaps followed by three large fields of handicappers. The mathematics are un-arguable: there was one way to win the Jackpot of around £80,000, compared with 1728 different ways of taking a share of a pool generating a payout (after deductions) of £350,000.

The Scoop6 bet

During 1998 and 1999, a series of meetings with some senior racing journalists resulted in the spawning of a new single bet, which has helped bring horserace betting and the Tote's name into greater public awareness at the start of the new century. The quid pro quo of excellent food and wine in return for honest advice from these professionals, many of whom were regular Tote punters, seemed a fair exchange. That the Tote Scoop6 – in which a winning bonus of more than £1.5 million could be gen-erated – should eventually come from these meetings and satisfy the long-expressed desire to find a 'superbet', delighted the participants.

The Scoop6, plainly, is not easy to win. The idea was to manufacture a prize which compares with the money to be won on the National Lottery, but with a mathematically feasible element – unlike the Lottery's multi-millions to one odds. Thus the £2 unit stake was initiated to make the bet less easy to win than the longstanding £1 Tote Jackpot. Sensible, too, was the decision to run the bet on Saturdays only, the day when most betting is transacted, and only covering six races live on television.

The original conception was that the BBC and Channel Four would share the TV coverage for the bet, but logistical factors soon predicated against the BBC's regular participation. BBC racing is generally placed at the start of the Saturday *Grandstand* programme, while Channel Four's coverage generally runs from mid-afternoon. Furthermore, the willingness of Channel Four to beef up its own coverage into a regular two-meeting event each week enabled the Tote to schedule the entire bet around that coverage, and the overnight switching, where possible, of less competitive races outside televised coverage also helped the bet.

The BBC had become inflexible, but the first signs of a change of heart on their part came with a switch of racing to BBC2 on international Six Nations rugby days. This had its downside for the BBC as viewing figures on their minor channel were even smaller than the regular figures achieved by Channel Four. The Tote reserves the right to break the informal monopoly to Channel Four, and such races as the Grand National and the Stewards' Cup at Goodwood's Glorious meeting are obvious possible vehicles to help maximise the potential of the Scoop6.

The bet has been cleverly framed, with a triple share-out after an initial deduction of 30 percent. The win pool on the day comprises another 25 percent; a further 25 percent goes to a place pool, with the remaining 20 percent going forward to the Bonus pool. The Bonus, which is also swelled by the full amount of any money bet into unwon win pools, is available to all the winners of any previous week's win pool.

Early in 2000, two Bonuses were contested with upwards of £1 million as the potential payout. In the first instance, a single winning ticket, shared by seven Munich-based racing fans, shot for a Warwick handicap chase but their horse ran poorly. Two weeks later, 19 winning tickets from the previous week brought some cooperation from the winners, at the instigation of Patrick Veitch, a professional backer. Having set in motion a plan for all the other ticket-holders to join in attacking an 18-runner handicap hurdle at Haydock, Veitch pulled out and selected Merry Masquerade, the favourite. The other 18 left one of the horses out of their bet and doubled on Merry Masquerade. At least that gave the group two-thirds of the total, but Veitch scooped more than half a million pounds when the favourite obliged.

The Tote was a little irritated initially that such collusion threatened the spirit of the bet; but then, probably at least half of the ticket-holders would have settled on the winner anyway, and the Bonus was therefore destined to stop after several months of building up.

The big payouts did one obvious thing. Racing and betting became a much more prominent item in newspaper and television coverage, and the level of Scoop6 activity was instantly enhanced.

The Trifecta bet

One of the biggest money-spinners on the American race-tracks is the Trifecta, a bet which requires the punter to select the first three home in the correct order in a given race. Most punters in the pari-mutuel queues favour this form of betting because dividends can be high.

British bookmakers have long offered a tricast, based on starting-price odds, while the Tote had the much less difficult to win Trio bet, where the punter still needed the first three horses but in any order. The Trio was a poor public relations medium, even though it had its adherents, because dividends looked small in comparison with the tricast offered in betting shops. The Trifecta bet was based originally on one race on each race day, but it was soon extended to all races with eight or more declared runners at the overnight stage.

The Tote management realised that this was spreading the jam over too large an area. Most pools on individual races were small, and very often no winner or only a part-winner was declared. The result was a wholesale carry forward to the next racing day. At the time of writing this bet was in urgent need of a rethink.

The Exacta bet

As with the Trifecta, American punters have grown up with the Exacta bet, in which two horses have to be nominated to finish first and second in the correct order. This bet has been the staple diet for US tracks and dividends can be high. Historically, the Tote has offered a Dual Forecast, where two horses are nominated to finish first and second, but in either order.

In January 2000 this bet was scrapped in favour of the Tote Exacta, which equates to its American namesake. The first few months of operation showed a constant overall edge against its betting-shop rival, the 'computer straight forecast' or CSF. Tote managers accept that this advantage can be minimised in some instances, notably where a long odds-on favourite beats a long-priced outsider, in which case the multiplier effect used for calculating the CSF makes that bet potentially more competitive.

New technology: friend or foe?

The Tote recently introduced new machines intended to facilitate the acceptance of bets. Where the staff are less than fully conversant with the technology there have been a number of snags with this. Queues at racetracks remain frustrating in many instances, and often there is more chance of winning the National Lottery than getting to the front of the queue in time to place a bet. Over the past few years, I have had my share of frustrations in this respect. Two that come most readily to mind were instances where only a small amount of money was involved.

One day at Leicester a few years ago, I had a bet (it might have been £20) on a novice chase. When my horse fell my ticket was discarded with the customary irritation, but unfortunately none of the horses had completed the course. Returning from the antiquated Leicester press room, where the sandwiches were both plentiful and nourishing (and the cups were of that foamy composition that makes tea, coffee and champagne taste equally unappetising), I was confronted by a scene of grown men scrabbling about on the floor in search of anything resembling a Tote ticket – one of those older-style small square card types. Needless to say, there was nothing close to where my ticket had been decanted, so I returned to the window at which I had placed my commission.

The friendly lady in red checked her screen and relayed the happy news that no ticket of the magnitude of £20 had been claimed for the horse in question. Helpfully, she further informed me that I should write to Tote House, in Putney, London, from where they would issue the original stake money within a matter of days. Six or seven weeks after the events at Leicester, a letter duly came from the Tote, informing me that no ticket of the unit stake on the horse I had backed remained unclaimed. The loss was, of course, my own fault, and the obvious advice is to keep all tickets until the final result is announced. The snag is that undestroyed tickets tend to remain in a remote pocket and are liable to be discovered at the next visit to the cleaners by a non-racing enthusiast with responsibility for such matters.

There is something about racing in the Midlands which sets it apart. A more recent example of a rare Tote mishap is the case of a non-bet of minuscule proportions. After having a bet in the ring at Towcester early in the new millennium, I noticed from a television screen that the horses were milling around at the start of a race at Wolverhampton. A quick look at my *Racing Post* revealed it was a contest involving some decent all-weather performers. I fancied King Priam to beat Weet-A-Minute and, feeling in my trouser pocket, unearthed three pound coins.

On my arrival at the head of the Tote queue there were still a few horses remaining to go into the stalls at Wolverhampton. I asked for a £3 Exacta and pushed the money over; whereupon one of the coins – they always seem to have a mind of their own – dropped down below the shelf with a bang. This event coincided with the intervention of a supervisor, who chose to distract his female colleague with a question unrelated to the more urgent task of servicing the queue. Then she glanced down at the shelf and, seeing two coins, asked: 'Is that one way or each way?' I replied that I had specified 'Exacta' from the start, and she proceeded to punch out a £2 bet – at which point I directed her attention to the third spherical object which had joined the assorted detritus below the shelf level. 'So you wanted a £3 Exacta, then?'

Now the Tote's rule on minimum bets kicked in. To get the £3 bet she first needed to cancel my initial £2 wager, a task she achieved with alacrity. A glance at the pictures from Wolverhampton brought the first moment of unease, not just for me, but for the hordes waiting behind urging her 'to get a move on'.

Meanwhile, she now proceeded to hit the wrong buttons once or twice in the more difficult task of placing the £3 Exacta, and even checked the board behind her which advised staff on what to do when accepting such a revolutionary new wager from the public. The supervisor tried to take a hand. The cashier seemed almost relieved when, on finally punching the correct sequence of buttons, she announced: 'Too late, I'm afraid', refunding the entire three coins. The supervisor quickly exited the converted chicken run in which they were housed, blissfully oblivious to the anxiety caused to myself and others in the queue.

Naturally, King Priam did get up in the last few yards to beat Weet-A-Minute. I didn't bother to complain, realising that if I had got the ill-starred bet on, some divine intelligence would have been transmitted to King Priam that under no circumstances should he go past Weet-A-Minute. That is the law of race betting for many – on some days at least – and you need to identify those days with alacrity. The Towcester bet, which fortuitously was of a more generous proportion, came up and all was well in the world once more.

Maybe the answer to these problems will be the introduction of all-encompassing self-service machines, such as are available for example in Japan and parts of the United States. At least then we should have only ourselves to blame for missed chances.

Under new management

In March 2000 the Home Secretary, Jack Straw, announced his decision to end the government's control of the Tote. A year earlier, Mr Straw had paved the way for its eventual privatisation, and several options were considered in the interim. The eventual decision to sell the Tote to a racing consortium had been the preferred option of its chairman Peter Jones, and of his fellow board members.

From its position of rapidly rising turnover, increasing in 1999 from just short of £400 million to nearly £500 million, the Tote made profits of £23 million, more than half of which was passed on to the racing industry in one way or another. Jones believes that the sale, when concluded, will enable the Tote to make a major contribution to the wealth and health of the whole of racing.

Betting on the Internet

It has been evident for many years that the old order in betting is unsatisfactory. In particular, deductions of 9 percent by bookmakers seems unreasonable in view of the margins already existing in on-course betting markets. Betting on the internet is now a reality and may increase betting turnover on horseracing.

Bookmaker Victor Chandler's move 'offshore' to Gibraltar in 1999 proved the catalyst for many apparently irreversible changes to the way betting is and will be conducted. Ladbrokes soon followed with an offshore arm, offering the same discounts on deductions available to Chandler clients. However, it was left to William Hill, of the three major firms, to offer the customer potentially the best deal of all.

John Brown, William Hill's boss, has been the most obstinate barrier to the embracing of Tote Direct throughout the industry (Ladbrokes and Coral are the players, as I mentioned earlier). While Hill's remain outside that grouping, Tote pools will stay smaller than is ideal. Brown is, however, more conventional on the matter of how much contribution bookmakers can afford under the Levy scheme, which has funded racing since betting shops were legalised in the early 1960s. Like his counterparts among bookmaking combines, Brown preaches the gospel that they cannot afford to pay any more into racing.

In early 2000, Brown masterminded a new internet betting site which enables punters to bet tax- or deduction-free via a sophisticated and informative site. In this scenario the entire element of general betting duty is picked up by Hills. Blue Square, another major internet bookmaker, was travelling down the same route in the weeks leading up to the Budget in March of 2000. So, from a position where the proportion of turnover diverted to racing could only inch agonisingly up to around 1.5 percent, suddenly these bookmakers were able to offset the full 9 percent deducted from betting-shop bets – and still pay the general betting duty of 6.75 percent.

Part of the reason for this is the fact that an increasing proportion of total betting is nowadays conducted on other sports, where bookmakers are not bothered with Levy payments. Margins on football betting are just over 13 percent, and such is the volume of that betting that it is easy to see how the duty to the government can be afforded.

Clearly, the problem area is the betting shops. Despite low wage levels, these shops are often situated in city-centre locations and are therefore very expensive to maintain. Internet betting systems reduce the unit cost markedly, so it is impossible to understand why book-making combines still want to make acquisitions in the betting-shop field.

William Hill's site early in 2000 was easily accessed and just as easily understood. Its design deserves high praise. The imaginative use of race sponsorship to advertise the site, and the tax-free element of the bets, reflect John Brown's marketing skill.

For example, William Hill's sponsorship of a major Ascot jumps race in February coincided with the first-ever internet broadcast of an English race meeting. The actual event chosen was the Mitsubishi Shogun Ascot Chase, a race which is significant in providing pointers for future Cheltenham Festival events and which was won, despite injury, by the improving Rockforce trained by Paul Nicholls.

The internet broadcast, using pictures from the BBC, attracted 23,000 computer users and confirmed that this embryonic but mushrooming market will help shape the way racing and betting develop in the coming years. The one certainty is that progressively more and more racing fans will wish to view on their computer screens, which will then adapt to their home television screens, on which the capability of betting and banking will also be married.

In the meantime, the issue of security of transactions will be paramount. Ladbrokes' site makes the potential user aware that he or she should be careful of the security element. Just as banks nowadays follow a process of security questioning before revealing any personal information over the telephone, so a series of financial transactions needs to be carefully secured to safeguard the customer (and the company). Computer fraud in general will be widespread, but such is the ability of the service providers and the police to identify fraudulent uses that betting via the internet should be made acceptably safe.

Most internet bets are placed, not on credit accounts, but via debit cards such as Delta, Switch or Electron. One logical outcome of the spread of internet betting will therefore be that the long-established legal principle that betting debts cannot be recoverable in law will disappear – except perhaps in the case of long-established arrangements with individual firms and customers. Whether banks will be happy for customers to transact a large proportion of their bets through their bank accounts will presumably depend on their rate of success!

As to benefits for the consumer, the first is the limitation to the deductions. If these no-tax concessions continue, probably at least in the short term, the punter will find that his or her betting budget lasts a little bit longer. Another benefit is that fewer bets are tending to be refused to punters who are paying 'up front' with debit cards.

The main hope for bookmakers, however, is that by widening the number of punters, and attracting new blood into what has been perceived as an ageing betting community both on and off course, overall activity will rise. The old guard has a limited betting budget. Over many years, the leisure pound has been dispersed widely around other activities, with films, restaurants and soccer matches offering very strong competition. Younger people with money to spend on racing are likely to be seduced into its ambit through an association like internet betting. There is no doubt that thrills of backing winners which can be seen on a domestic screen may well produce new, relatively wealthy, racing enthusiasts.

It is the younger element that Ladbrokes – slowly away

as far as getting into internet betting was concerned – has targeted, and wisely so. The middle-aged person who belatedly discovers that there are such things as computers will always struggle to understand their workings. The younger generation, computer-literate to a large degree, can surf around the new technologies with great facility, and this fluency is part of the attraction for the internet site provider.

For horseracing there could be a downside. Ladbrokes is pushing the football betting element, perhaps to the detriment of racing because of the stated intention of not making any contribution to racing from internet bets.

Bookmakers Offshore

In any major industry, it can take only an apparently minor alteration in trading conditions to transform, for the better or indeed for the worse, the fortunes of the participants.

The betting industry differs from many others in that, while taxation is calculated on the basis of levels of turnover, those levels do not absolutely reflect the true amount of money available to backers. The equation between winning and losing bets decides the punter's overall situation. To win over the long term, he could invest more than twenty times the actual amount of disposal money with which he can afford to bet. Likewise, a small loss can result from many individual transactions.

That, to a degree, is similar to the situation for the

stock market and money market player. However, while most small shareholders tend to identify a prospective stock or share in which to invest over the medium or long term, the punter is generally in a win or bust state for each wager.

Under the old order, it is easy to see how a punter's betting bank could be dissipated even when the individual is relatively successful. Taking a notional £1000 betting bank and concentrating on backing only even-money chances in £100 units, the erosion because of the tax element is rapid and debilitating, as the following shows.

Suppose his first bet is £100, tax pre-paid, on a winner. He thus stakes £100 plus £9 and receives £200 in return, for a net win of £91. His next bet is also a gross £109, but on a loser, so after two bets he is already £18 down. If he continues in similar vein – and that in relative terms would comfortably exceed the success rate of most tipsters – over a period of just 110 bets he would be broke, all bar £10. For him to lose that £990, he has also contributed £990 to the combined government duty and racing Levy, and has given the bookmaker a little windfall too.

But from a total disposable budget of £1000, he has actually contributed 6.75 percent general betting duty of a total of £11,000, which realises the handsome sum of £742.50 to the taxman. In other words, with that high level of successful wagers, his bank generates around 75 percent in true monetary terms.

Victor Chandler's decision to go offshore in 1999 came from a realisation by this far-seeing entrepreneur that the Far East was a fertile ground for high-level punters. Singapore and Hong Kong had been his primary source of new, large-volume punters, with North Americans also proving important for betting on their own special sports, like American football and basketball.

Chandler, the leading rails bookmaker and son of another doyen in the betting ring, the late Victor Chandler senior, discovered by experience that football betting had become a massive market. Premier League matches had proved an obvious magnet as they were, and still are, televised live in both Singapore and Hong Kong, not just on Sky Sports' regular Sunday afternoon and Monday night slots, but also on Saturdays. The occasional Far East football betting specialist could be investing amounts equivalent to a large proportion of the overall take at some race meetings where Chandler was the highest-profile rails bookmaker.

Understandably, the Far East punters balked at paying a 9 percent deduction on a betting medium in which margins were already ten percentage points or more against them already. By moving almost his entire operation to Gibraltar, Chandler was able to operate his football business on a tax-free basis for these clients and avoid the chance that high tax deductions in the UK would cause them to look elsewhere.

With horseracing, Chandler agreed to pay a voluntary 3 percent contribution to racing. Needless to say, the Levy Board and other prominent members of racing's various authorities were quick to complain when they perceived that he had failed to honour that spontaneous offer. For Chandler's part, the firm has greatly increased its sponsorships of horseraces around Britain, and for anybody to complain about the way it helps British racing, albeit while advertising own branding, is little short of impertinent.

There are many instances of major firms and individuals leaving Britain on a full-time basis to avoid the full weight of the country's tax regime. In Chandler's case, his move was designed to illustrate the fact that the level of government duty was excessive and a barrier to the growth of betting revenue. Chandler quickly increased his level of clients once he moved to Gibraltar, and the provision of a free 08000 phone number to place bets was another commercially astute move to maximise his advantage.

As with all technology, the competition will inevitably catch up, but Chandler will rightly be the beneficiary of the best of the clients, as well as the well-earned accolade of being a pathfinder through what had been tricky waters. While Ladbrokes were quickly establishing their own Gibraltar base to be added to the long-established domestic office in Harrow, West London, Victor Chandler was developing an internet betting site, although retaining a small credit and course operation in London to cater for his more traditional clients.

Let's now revisit the betting example worked out above. The Chandler horseracing client who matches his 9 percent rival by alternating even-money winners and losers from a £1000 bank will be laughing. Using the same formula, it would take him 333 bets to dispose of his bank. If the British government ever decided to reduce general betting duty to anywhere close to 3 percent, it is possible – but by no means certain – that the offshore firms could be enticed back home.

Unlike petrol and cigarette taxations, which only marginally influence consumption as they have a linear or arithmetic effect, tax on betting is of a geometric nature so a cut in the rate would produce much greater upwards elasticity of demand. That is the opinion, not only of myself, but of the authors of a major study of betting published during the early months of 2000, which concluded that a betting explosion would result.

That we can be talking in these terms, given the intransigence of both government and bookmakers over the years, is merely another reason for being grateful to Victor Chandler. He was the necessary daring visionary who was required to lead the way, and enabling the racing and other betting businesses to become dynamic and adapt to the requirements of punters in the twenty-first century.

Spread betting

In the early 1990s a number of firms that had specialised in betting on stock market indices saw the opportunity to extend that form of wagering to horseracing and other sports. As with most trading positions it was possible to identify a buying and selling price for anything, and the margin between was, and ever is, the broker's profit.

Spread betting on racing and sport was set up under the same financial rules that regulate stock and share buying, and so losses incurred in such betting are recoverable in law, unlike traditional credit betting with bookmakers.

The major firms now deal in several sports, as well as in politics and current affairs. The horseracing market contracts are offered in what are termed 'ticks', which are margins reflecting superiority. Betting can be conducted on starting prices, where the 'tick' represents a tenth of the starting price, as well as on distances and matches (horse A against horse B) – and in each case the 'tick' is then one-tenth of a length.

Three firms, City Index, Sporting Index and IG Index, dominated spread betting from an early point. Considering that spread betting is not an activity in which I am even an occasional participant, it is perhaps surprising that apparently I played a minor part in popularising the activity in a horseracing context.

Buying and selling: the Dettori bet

One day, approaching the start of the 1994 Flat season I called my friend Wally Pyrah who had just moved from his job at Coral to become the PRO for Sporting Index. The latter firm, under Compton Hellyer, was trying to force its way into the forefront ahead of the early sector leader City Index with its inspirational boss, Jonathan Sparke.

The reason for my call was that leading jockey Frankie Dettori had decided that year to mount a serious challenge for the Jockeys' Championship – which in those days was based on all domestic winners throughout the year, including all-weather racing in the period leading up to the start of turf racing on the Flat in March. Nowadays the all-weather circuit, in which the leading jockeys generally do not compete regularly, has its own winter championship running from mid-November until late March.

At the time of my call to Pyrah, Dettori had made a flying start and was already pushing 50 winners. I enquired about the spread for Dettori winners for the entire year, to be told that no actual market had been set up but it could be fixed at 164–169.

In spread betting there are buyers and sellers. In the above market, if you believed that Dettori would finish with more than 169 winners, you would be a buyer. If, on the other hand you believed he could not manage 164 winners, you would then be a seller. The five points in between is the operator's profit margin. Whether buying or selling, the profit or loss calculation relates to a multiple of one's unit stake. Thus, for a £10 unit say, the potential for loss and indeed profit can be great, and the unwitting punter could be landed in much more trouble than bargained for.

In early 1994, however, the Dettori market seemingly could have only one result for Sporting Index. I wrote an article in the *Daily Telegraph* the next day on their Dettori offer, suggesting that the position was almost certainly understating Dettori's winning chances for the year – adding that, barring accidents, it was hard to see how he could ride fewer than 200 winners (in the event he amassed 233.)

I have never held a spread betting account – there are too many other complications to life – so I called colleague Jim McGrath, now BBC TV's brilliant race commentator, and told him about the Sporting Index Dettori market. I suggested that he might want to help himself to some of the action. Jim agreed that it looked a good possibility and offered to go the same for me.

The *Telegraph* article duly appeared, and as soon as the phones opened at Sporting Index that March morning they were inundated with punters trying to get on. One big feature of spread betting is its immediacy, so once the firm saw the way the demand lay it quickly adjusted its offer upwards by around 50 winners.

Those of us lucky enough to have guessed or projected correctly were instantly in the position of being able to call in their profit without the actual race being run. Jim duly closed his deal and we ended up with a grand each for our £20 unit stake. On the other hand, those punters who had believed Dettori would not make 164, and therefore sold, would have been in an instant crippling deficit situation. Apparently, according to Pyrah, 'there were very few if any of those'.

New challenges

Spread betting has come on a lot since those innocent, unsophisticated days. Every day, racing markets are traded on racecard numbers, aggregate starting prices, matches between nominated horses, aggregate winning distances, favourites, jockeys and heavyweights, among others.

The racecard numbers market is determined by the addition of all the saddle-cloth numbers of the winning horses on a day's programme. Most firms then double the total number, presumably to widen the potential of the market. If high-numbered – and therefore lightly weighted – horses win most races, the settling figure, known as the 'make-up', will be high. On days when there are small fields, and the top horses on the card predominate, the make-up will be low. At the major meetings, these markets are highly volatile, with big fields offering the potential for large wins or losses.

Match bets are straightforward enough. The spread firms select two horses in a given race, often with an apparently similar chance, and offer a superiority margin between them, expressed as an amount in lengths. For deciding the outcome, margins for distances less than a length are generally accepted as 0.1 of a length for a short head; 0.2 for a head; 0.3 for a neck, and so on for the accepted margins thereafter. A punter correctly calling a 'buy' for horse A over horse B will receive the number of lengths of that superiority (make-up) in winnings for each unit of the bet. If wrong, the punter loses a similar amount, also taking into account the spread bookmaker's own margin.

Distance bets are run on similar rules to match bets. The total of the individual winning distances of a day's racing at a single meeting determines the make-up figure. In jumping, the potential margins are much larger, so to cap the possible wide fluctuations the spread firms usually operate with a 12-length maximum margin for a single Flat race and 30 lengths as the maximum individual margin for a jumps contest.

There was initially much conjecture among racing professionals that some jockeys might have an unhealthy interest in the spread market on distance betting. It did, for a while, appear that in some races the winners were pushed right out even when a long way clear, while a rider on the prospective runner-up seemed less vigorous. In other instances, horses with an overwhelming apparent superiority were constrained to win by the minimum of margins. While it is likely that such actions might be approved by owners and trainers hoping not to have their horses severely treated in future handicaps, there was speculation that hidden agendas might be involved. Happily, those misgivings have since been largely dispelled.

In favourites spread betting the normal formula is that each favourite at a given meeting is awarded 25 points if it wins; 10 points if it finishes second and 5 points for third. A day of winning favourites, especially on what had seemed an open, competitive card beforehand, would make for large winners and losers.

In jockeys spread betting, the same points for winners, seconds and thirds are used as in favourites betting. To avoid arguments about jockeys not actually riding points-scoring horses for which they had been intended riders according to morning newspapers, for the purposes of this bet such points are credited to the nominated jockey.

The heavyweights spread betting market concerns the horses on a day's race card carrying the number 1 on their saddle-cloths. Again the '25–10–5' points formula is used to determine the final make-up figure.

It is probably fair to say that most regular spread punters confine themselves to some sensible wagering on distances and favourites, concentrating on the days when a stiff track and soft going promise wide-margin winners and the increased likelihood of beaten favourites.

Spread sports betting

As spread betting developed, its adaptations for other sports soon became more sophisticated. Superiority indices for one soccer team over another, principally for Premier League, cup or major international events like the World Cup, have produced a betting bonanza. The margins are expressed in decimal points of goals. Examples of other markets are the time to the first goal, shirt numbers of goal scorers, numbers of corners, and bookings and red cards.

In cricket, runs scored individually by players, and total team runs – in single matches or over a Test series say – were obvious market vehicles. But it was in another cricket market that the biggest killing against the spread firms occurred.

The 1999 Cricket World Cup was staged in England at a time of the year, the spring, when the teams were in varying degrees of preparedness. The number of teams was bolstered in the early stages by such cricketing minnows as Holland, Scotland, Bangladesh and Kenya. The market for the number of wide deliveries was set by the spread firms at a level which, considering the number of matches, might have been appropriate if the protagonists had been confined to the major Test-playing countries, but actually vastly understated the potential for wides.

The early group matches, staged when many of the teams had not yet played themselves in, brought an unbelievable number of inept displays from bowlers, and in some cases wicket-keepers. This situation was magnified by the corresponding harsh application by the umpires of the unwritten law on one-day wides, especially for balls going marginally leg-side. In a matter of days, the index was raised abruptly. Some punters made massive profits. Others, less lucky, were stung.

The whole episode was great publicity for the spread firms, but it told punters most eloquently that the risks of spread betting on such potentially volatile markets can be immense.

CHAPTER FOUR

Betting Strategies

There are two types of punter: in short, winners and losers. In those categories, however, clearly there are varied ways of operating. Disciplined backers have a much better chance than the do-or-die optimist, but the element of luck does take a hand.

Of all the punters I have known, Angus Loughran – famed for his Statto contributions to television's Fantasy Football show, and now a *Daily Telegraph* columnist and BBC's racing betting pundit – is the luckiest. Like many 'lucky' people, however, he works harder at the job than anyone else. His life is an endless sequence of air and rail travel as he attends many important soccer, golf, snooker and cricket matches as well as the racing. He'll be in place at the Tuesday opening of the Cheltenham Festival. That night he'll fly out to Milan or Barcelona for a European Champions League match the following day, and then there he'll be again, one of the first to arrive in the press room on Gold Cup day, whatever the travel difficulties he has to overcome.

I reckon some of his luck is outrageous, but his knowledge is encyclopaedic and he ranks as an excellent soccer commentator for EuroSport. The oft-quoted remark of Gary Player, 'the harder I practice, the luckier I get', applies equally to Angus. The most compelling thing is his generosity of spirit to friends and colleagues, while much of his travelling is done without any support from an employer, but for his own enlightenment.

Loughran comes from a younger generation of sports watcher, and his wide knowledge proves the fact that you do not necessarily need to have performed well in a given sport to commentate on or write about it with authority. One of the younger faces on the scene is Mike Vince, whose build might suggest that his participation in sports has been of an imagined rather than actual nature; but he is another whose intensive research has produced benefits and a burgeoning broadcasting career.

Betting on anything but a minimal recreational scale is a serious business. As time has gone on the betting opportunities have widened, and even those most adroit bookies who once would have stopped every regular winning punter from betting with them have adjusted to the new order.

First principles

There cannot be anything easier than losing money at the races, especially when betting on credit. There is nothing worse, for example, than having an open-ended betting account, starting out with the ambition of winning say £100, and ending up betting in much larger units simply to retrieve a position. Effectively, that means that from a situation where you would have been happy to achieve a small potential win of a few pounds, you can eventually face the prospect of a massive loss. That, to me, seems to be the margin that credit firms have over ill-advised, impulsive punters: the guy who gets a little behind and thrashes about trying anything to get level will inevitably become a massive loser in the longer term.

Many years ago, when betting on an account, I ran up a long losing sequence with a bookmaker. Then, one Easter bank holiday, well aware that I had gone way beyond the nominal limit on the account, I selected a multiple bet around the mounts of Declan Gillespie, later one of Ireland's best jockeys and now a successful trainer there. This day he put together a string of winners. Had the successful bet been honoured, I would have been several thousand pounds to the good. The passage of time has told me that the bookmaker was right to refuse a payout because the bet had been accepted in error. Many times since, however, losing bets in such circumstances with other firms have been allowed to stand!

Principle 1: Decide how much you can afford to lose over a given period

If you intend going to the track rather than bet in a betting shop or from home, obviously the cost element is a major factor. Compared with racing in other countries, racing in Britain is expensive. The main enclosure, the Members, usually costs between £14 and £20 for admission, and for some of the festivals – Royal Ascot, Cheltenham and Goodwood for instance – that can rise to £50 a day. Clearly those occasions must be treated separately, perhaps more as social outings, in which case you will be able to justify the extra cost.

Rail and car travel is increasingly costly. So, too, despite the efforts of some tracks to rein in their caterers' prices, is food and drink. On the track these are rarely as competitive as in comparable high street restaurants and pubs. Thus it is clear that the racegoer must treat the day out as an equivalent activity to theatre-going, football or a visit (if you must) to the Millennium Dome.

The betting must be kept separate. If you win at the races and it costs you £50 as a couple for the day out, against £100 if you had broken level or £150 if you lost, that would seem fine. Never go racing expecting to win anything: you should be delighted if you return home having defrayed some of the day's expenses. If you arrive home with more than you started, you are free to assume you are one of the very few experts and muse that if you'd gone to see a musical or to Highbury, that would not have been the case.

The best formula to eventual 'success' (a small reduction in overall losses can be so treated) is to nominate a set amount of money to be used as a betting bank. In conjunction – and this is the hard part – you will need to keep a strict record of all bets placed; more of that later.

Most people going racing will know that if there are seven races on the card and they intend betting only at the meeting they attend, and their betting allowance is £100, then they have £10 or £15 to bet on each race.

Occasional punters are more disciplined in such circumstances than the betting shop regular who arrives at a racecourse and behaves as he does in the high street. This chap can have the same £100 to spend. In the first race he sees a hot favourite that he reckons will start at 5-4 against. 'If I can get that price,' he tells himself, 'I'll have £40 on to win fifty.'

When the betting opens, other people clearly have the same opinion of the horse, which opens at 6-4 *on*. The predictable move from the impulsive punter is to try still to win roughly what he would have originally expected from this first bet. While he stands there thinking 'Shall I have £60 on it to win forty?', the price disappears as the other punters rush in. Before he looks round, the horse's price has shortened to 7-4 on. He still wants to win somewhere close to the amount he had in his mind to set the day rolling; so he ups his stake to £70 to win £40 – and then watches the horse lose.

In a twinkling the anticipated £150 of betting money for the rest of the card has shrunk to £30 and, even if some of his other selections win, I guarantee he will go home broke. Believe me, I've been there and (as they say) bought the T-shirt, which naturally no longer fits.

What happens next is that the following selection, which might also have appeared an obvious favourite at 7-4 on, could well be offered at nearly even money. Our hero, however, is into the alternative strategy of looking for an outsider to retrieve the £70 before he can start again. He finds a 10-1 shot, which runs a blinder and looks the probable winner until the favourite catches him in the last 100 yards and everyone says 'What a price!'

This little tale demonstrates the difference between

the 'unlucky' punter and the Angus Loughran model. Angus might have looked at the first horse and decided that, because it was at far shorter odds than he had expected, he would either miss altogether, or just have a minimal bet. You have to have an idea of when it is in your interests to bet. When the level of potential winnings is outweighed by the amount of possible loss and the two elements are out of proportion with the probability of success, the Angus type will step back. This is the foundation of the concept of 'value' in betting, of which more later.

There is, nonetheless, plenty of scope to win money at racing. In general terms, the racecourse bookie who keeps paying out to the same successful punter will not mind provided he makes his overall profit. This is true simply because so many other punters are ill-informed, undisciplined and live in a wonderland where, as long as the occasional bet collects, they are self-deluded 'winners' and excellent form judges.

Anybody arriving at the decision to become serious about betting will need to be very careful about his or her betting bank. Experience has shown that even if I stick to a single selection the capacity for long losing runs is a constant possibility. That hard-earned experience has taught me that betting at level stakes – or at least with that as a basis – may not be exciting but it reduces the overall risk.

Betting can be treated as an alternative to operating in the stock markets. Admittedly, if a bet loses all the stake goes, whereas share fluctuations rarely leave the shareholder with a stock of nil worth. But any regular dabbler in that area knows that even the most solid-looking share investment can succumb to the momentum of a bear market at any time.

A betting bank should ideally, in my view, be operated in units of £10, as that enables a punter at any level of activity to raise or lower the unit stake and still have a pattern to work with. The ideal total for a betting bank is £300, that is 30 units of £10 each.

Losing runs are the bane of all punters, and for that matter newspaper tipsters like myself. Even in successful seasons, it is possible for my daily nap selection – my best bet of the day – to contain sequences of losers well into double figures. A bank run on too short a sequence, say ten bets, is liable to be extinguished very rapidly and there is not always the ability for an individual to replenish and start again. Even 20 bets can be inadequate, especially when the punter does not restrict operations to a few selective wagers.

It is particularly rewarding when a £300 bank produces a good profit early in its existence. In this case, the punter has two options. He may either pocket the early profit and start again with a brand new £300 bank, or he can simply start from scratch with a higher bank that includes the profit. Thus if he has taken the bank to £450, each of his 30 individual bets can be raised to £15. In either case, he is starting to play with the enemy's money and it is surprising just how much can be generated from small starting points, given selectivity and hard work.

Naturally there is the other standpoint. Should the entire £300 be exhausted in a short time, either through injudicious or over-frequent betting, that punter should re-examine his methods. The random approach – be it to concentrate support on a specific trainer, jockey or owner, or on market movements, or even on newspaper tipsters – is not recommended as a single method.

Research shows that while some tipsters do better than others, even the most successful generally show a significant loss to level stakes on all selections. Some newspaper tipsters have actually achieved an overall winning figure to level stakes on all tips in a given year, but Sod's Law prescribes that the day you follow that successful column, it will draw blank.

Principle 2: Keep records

The prospect of having to enter all the bets you have made during the period of operating a betting bank may seem daunting or plain futile. You go to the track with so much, you spend so much on food and other expenses, and come home with so much. You win or you lose.

Maybe so. But then, what about that little ante-post bet you placed and conveniently forgot when the horse was withdrawn lame? And then there was the stop-off at the betting shop when you had a small yankee in the morning, and then the Switch bet you had with one of the big firms from the office the day before. The easiest thing in betting is to convince yourself that you have actually done better than is really the case. Just a one-week trial of keeping records can be instrumental in turning a habitual loser into a potential regular winner.

A small book – in which you can list the date, name of horse, stake and return (if any) together with a running tally – will provide the key. That information can be translated easily to a spreadsheet on a computer and provide comprehensive evidence of the time of the year when your betting is at its most effective and when it is probably wise to reduce activity.

Such evidence is also helpful in identifying in which type of race you are most successful and where you should avoid certain types of bet. If there is room, the trainer, jockey and track on which the bet is made can also be included, to provide further data to illuminate your strategy.

Principal 3: Decide your betting profile

As the previous chapter showed, the ways in which it is possible to place bets has widened rapidly in recent years. The traditional ways of betting have been supplemented by debit, internet, offshore and spread betting, on horses and other sports. Credit betting remains the one area where bets, unfairly to my mind, cannot be recovered in law. Betting shop and course punters, with bookmakers or the Tote, naturally put their cash down. Most observers contend that the days when betting debts should not be recoverable in law are long past because circumstances in society are far different.

With the debit card betting systems and internet betting, bets are backed by a card and the money is taken out of that particular account at point of sale. The fact that this gives the bookmaker a guarantee of payment by the punter has led the major firms to be rather more relaxed about which bets and stakes they are prepared to accept.

The punter will also find a more relaxed approach to his or her custom on the racecourse. Recent changes pushed through by the National Joint Pitch Council (NJPC) have been accompanied by much controversy, but have clearly provided major competitive benefits to the on-course market.

Credit accounts are likely to be overtaken as automation develops further. Bets will be placed via televisions linked to home computers and the relevant races watched in the comfort of one's living room. In the meantime, where an overall betting strategy is being developed, my view is that any existing credit account should be reserved for the emergency situation. This could be when you are unable to get to the track or a betting shop, or to your computer. Then there might be an occasional special bet when a horse you fancy for a major race is offered by that particular bookmaker at a highly attractive price.

So my contention is that the credit account should remain a reserve rather than a major sphere of activity. Traditionally, ante-post bets are not settled, either way, until the event has been run, and regular ante-post punters run the risk of running up considerable potential losses. The debit method of placing such bets seems preferable for that reason.

Principle 4: Look for value

If a regular punter on horseracing hopes to last for any length of time, relying on personal judgement rather than someone else's, he will need to grasp the tricky concept of 'value'. As we saw in the previous chapter, odds

are framed by the bookmaker on the basis of a one-
hundred percent total 'book'. It is evident that if his
'product' – in other words his range of odds on a single
race – are framed heavily in his favour, then his likely
percentage profit will be high. If the odds are framed in
the punter's favour, then the potential will be for a deficit
to the bookmaker.

Odds depend on many things. If a track has a large
number of punters, and plenty of on-course bookmakers,
the element of competition comes in strongly. Because
the odds are displayed on the individual boards, the dis-
cerning, quick-on-his-feet punter can often beat the odds,
especially in the case of a price for an individual horse
shortening.

At tracks like Ascot, the boards bookmakers in Tattersalls enclosure can extend for almost a furlong in front of
the main stand, and prices at either end can vary quite
considerably. In the old days a few 'bandits', operating
on the fringes, simply concentrated on the 'mug' money,
which is readily available from certain sections of the betting crowd at some special meetings. The coachloads of
day-trippers dressed in their best fashions and descend-
ing on the Silver Ring for Royal Ascot's four days in June,
and the once-a-year racegoers who attend the Hill on
Derby Day at Epsom, are especially liable to be uncritical
of very short prices from such bookmakers.

On a daily basis, however, these fringe bookies will
find it less easy to dupe the regulars, who have now come
to expect much better margins than was the case ten
years or so ago. Generally, like the once-a-year punters
they fleece, these rogue bookies do not appear until such

days, and the NJPC has them targeted as unwelcome in modern-day racing.

In the years from the 1970s until the betting-ring changes pushed through by the NJPC, a regular feature of betting rings in England was the frequency with which the major firms – led by Ladbrokes, but also William Hill and Coral on a smaller scale – were able to manipulate the prices in the ring by sending money back from their off-course offices. This was designed to depress odds available about well-backed or popular trainer–jockey combinations. The market at some tracks would be so weak that relatively little money could make dramatic differences to the odds available.

This situation, much to the irritation of some off-course combines, is no longer true because of the arrival of new, adventurous protagonists in the business. The old order smacked almost of insider trading, and in other industries might have been construed to contain elements of conflict of interest.

Tracks like Ascot, Kempton and Sandown, which attract a London audience, have tended to be the most competitive. Margins to the bookmakers at some of the better jumping meetings early in 2000 were down to around 10 percent, an alarming rate for off-course firms whose high costs of providing a comprehensive shop service have made them and their profits vulnerable to the reduced margins.

A regular working level of deduction of 10 percent could eventually be achievable for all meetings. Add to this either a nil deduction or a reduced one along the lines of the 3 percent imposed by Victor Chandler on his offshore service, then the punter clearly will have a better chance than at any time since the 1960s.

To spot an especially good value position, the punter needs to have a solid knowledge of the sport and an understanding of how to calculate odds – the latter is covered in the previous chapter. It is also helpful to compare the prices available from several bookmakers where they offer early or morning prices, or alternatively study the forecast odds in the *Racing Post*. Sometimes, a horse will be offered in the ring at much shorter odds than the newspapers or early odds predict. This could be because the morning price has been taken, or because the word on the track is that the horse has shown plenty at home.

The benefit to the bookmakers of providing early-morning betting shows is obvious. This is one instance where their prices can be displayed and provide a barometer of what might happen when the general betting gets under way later in the day. The big firms will happily accept a small bet at long odds from a noted insider at a successful stable, which houses a certain horse. Such a bet will have more significance than a heavy bet from a random punter without any known connections. The former instance will enable the bookmaker to take remedial action by reducing the price offered. 'Inspired money', though, generates a following and the mere act of reducing a price in a sphere where people are looking for clues often generates its own momentum and attracts further support.

British bookmakers are usually cautious on morning prices. Their margins tend to be higher than might be available in the betting ring during the afternoon, and generally more horses lengthen from their morning odds than shorten.

Some leading Irish bookmakers bet on all the English races on the day from early in the morning. They tend to be unwilling to take large bets, and again they get a virtually free feel of what could be coming at them later in the day. To show just how helpful this can be, I relate a tale of an incident concerning a fancied newcomer for a race at Newcastle early in 2000.

The horse in question had been working well and was primed for a run in a bumper race. He was an outsider in the *Racing Post* of that Saturday morning and, briefly, connections entertained hopes that he could start at long odds. Then an associate of one of the insiders, a bank manager if you please, chose to explore internet and Irish firms to see what price might be available, and was first on that morning. He was quoted 25-1, took those odds to £50 each way and sat back expecting a big pay-out.

Then the little snowball turned, appropriately for the time of year, into something of an avalanche, so that when the market settled down at Newcastle he was second favourite at 4-1. So the hapless connections were left with a terrible price, while their computer-literate associate could reckon on a handsome 5-1 for just the place part of his bet. In the event, Sod's Law was invoked by way of the horse getting a moderate ride from his inexperienced jockey to be a fast-finishing fourth, so nobody won except the bookies.

These odds reductions, however, do not necessarily imply poor value, and the best way to judge the horse may be in the paddock at the track. In our case, on-the-spot analysis suggested the horse would run well. In general terms, such judgement will need to be backed by knowledge, which can only be gained by regular racecourse attendance and careful scrutiny of horses before they run.

Just as some horses will be available at much shorter prices than anticipated, others could be much longer. Sometimes a stable whose winners tend to be well backed can be out of form and a number of well-supported horses might have run poorly. In these circumstances an 'obvious' favourite could be 'friendless in the market'. In a case like this, the value of a pre-race look in the paddock is especially important: if the horse looks a little lifeless or its coat is dull, that could confirm the view that it is an unlikely winner.

However, should that horse be bright and bouncy beforehand, and look fit and hard-muscled, with a glowing coat, the case for a speculative bet is strengthened. An expected 6-4 could stretch as far as 3-1, such can be the volatility of the betting market. Here, obviously, true value is clearly available. Judgement of value depends on analysing all the elements, starting with the odds, and expressing the probable chance (on your analysis) as a comparison with the actual odds.

The issue of value suggests another look at my normal advice of maintaining level stakes for day-to-day betting. In such cases, it can and indeed should be adjusted. If a supermarket announces a particularly attractive half-price offer, many shoppers are certain to take up whatever they need at the bargain figure. In racing, strangely, the tendency for many punters – like our chap who unwisely lost much of his £100 bank on a short-shot – is to increase their stake when the price is poor. The motivation for this is that, having envisaged a possible profit, a punter is unable to accept that the chosen animal is not a good betting proposition.

Like the half-price supermarket offer, a horse available at double the expected odds should be snapped up. My general rule of thumb is that I will double the usual stake if the price is significantly better than expected, while if a horse is too short I will either reduce the stake or not get involved at all.

At least if a horse wins and you haven't backed it because you were unwilling to take 'under the odds', you still have the consolation of knowing your opinion of the horse was right. When such a bad-value horse loses and you *have* backed it, all you have left is a hole in your pocket and the knowledge that you should not have been involved.

Ante-post betting

The heyday of ante-post betting has long gone. Bookmakers are too cute to risk much on being caught out in a world where betting opportunities are so much greater than in the old days.

In the immediate post-war years – now half a century and more away – the Derby, Grand National, Lincoln Handicap and one or two other events like Newmarket's Cambridgeshire and Cesarewitch comprised most of the ante-post activity during the year. The two handicap doubles, in the spring (Lincoln/National) and the autumn (Cambridgeshire/Cesarewitch), have virtually disappeared as a regular winter and summer activity for punters, while the big Cheltenham races, and long-term betting on the two Guineas classics, have strengthened in importance.

Whereas on-course margins are narrowing, the ante-post lists have become more strongly in favour of the bookies. Rarely are horses offered at bigger than 50-1 in many of these long-range events, whereas horses are offered at 100-1 on a daily basis at the track. It is an inescapable conclusion that these races are for the book-makers more 'shop window' than serious business, and there is a tendency for horses' prices to be cut abruptly without much actual punting activity.

In some cases, though, it is possible to understand the reluctance of the layers to compose proper ante-post books. Trainer Martin Pipe, for example, regularly makes multiple entries for major jump races, and is routinely reticent about which will run, until the money is down at least.

The lure of ante-post has thus become much less appealing to me. In 1999, my ante-post win on Oath for the Vodafone Derby, however, was the example of where obvious potential, coupled with a little inside knowledge, brought a value situation. A price of 16-1 after he won the Dee Stakes at Chester, backed by optimistic noises from owner and trainer, were the right components for a nice little touch.

Tote opportunities

The expansion in types of Tote bet has been a recent feature, headed by the Scoop6. Thinking of the latter, however, it is hard to suggest that there will ever be a set of circumstances for the punter in which a bet with a £2 unit requiring six winners can ever be considered good value.

There is precious little day-to-day value also in the normal win and place pools on the Tote. Many minor meetings produce small pools in which the majority of betting is focused on a few horses, especially those ridden by the leading jockeys. At the major meetings, however, where there are large, competitive fields, there is the prospect of very big prices. Horses offered at 33-1 in the ring could be available as much as four times that on the Tote at meetings like the Cheltenham Festival or Royal Ascot, particularly in the 30-horse fields which sprinkle those meetings.

The Tote Exacta, introduced in early 2000, replaced the under-performing Dual Forecast and has invigorated an area in which the Tote had been weak. In its first few months' existence, the Exacta increased turnover by 40 percent compared with its predecessor. It is easy to see why, as dividends have been superior to those of the bookmakers' computer straight forecast (CSF), the payout on which is based on starting prices. For the Exacta, I like to select a couple of fancied horses together with two more medium- or longer-priced horses. In all this comes to 12 bets, and the potential is for a big dividend, especially if the two less-fancied animals fill the first two places.

The Placepot has been the biggest money-spinner for the Tote, the appeal for the regular punter being the fact that it is (or should be) rather easier to win than the Jackpot. The value opportunity comes during some of the big meetings, when betting shop punters actually get an edge over racecourse backers in that they can have multiple bets in units of a single penny. Sometimes at Cheltenham or Royal Ascot, where the pools reach a quarter of a million pounds on a single day, multiples combining fancied runners and outsiders can enable the punter to crack some obscure problems.

The Trifecta is the least successful of the Tote's newer products, but there is one circumstance when it is worth an occasional crack. On most days the regular Trifecta pool tends to be small, so it often passes forward to a race on the following day. Some of these races attract money from up to a dozen single unwon pools, and any punter coming in on the feeder race is betting at favourable odds. That said, I will be surprised if the Trifecta is not re-modelled in the near future.

All-weather value

Winter racing on the turf can sometimes proceed untroubled by the weather. In those circumstances, the fact that there is insufficient strength in depth leaves much of the regular diet of jump racing starved of runners, especially in more valuable races. Favourites can be very short-priced and, considering the potential risks posed by the hurdles and fences, may represent poor value. There is sometimes more point, and certainly more potential for successful betting, in the intensive nine-week spell of all-weather racing which begins in the New Year and concludes a week before the Cheltenham Festival.

Of the three all-weather tracks – Lingfield, Wolverhampton and Southwell – I have enjoyed most success at Lingfield. Its Equitrack surface is the fastest of the three and seems to favour good-ground animals. It is soon easy to identify a horse that is suited to Lingfield (and indeed the other two tracks). In the way of such things, these regular winners can often be priced much more attractively as they go through the winter season than their achievements would indicate.

The all-weather racing was originally intended as a standby in case of lost fixtures on the turf in midwinter, and indeed in its early years more jump meetings were staged on the artificial surface. The relatively warm winters of recent years, combined with the success of all-weather in its own right, have altered the perspective – especially of owners and trainers for whom prize money compares well with that available to jumpers.

The new code has been responsible for enabling a number of younger trainers to develop their skills. Nick Littmoden, who started life as an instructor at the Southwell school for jockeys originally headed by former trainer Derek Kent, is the most prominent. He soon turned his attention to training horses, first at Southwell, and then as the in-house trainer at Wolverhampton, the newest of the three tracks. He quickly became a regular winner, and that success enabled him to take over Julie Cecil's Southbury Stables in Newmarket's Hamilton Road when she retired from training in 1998.

Littmoden, Karl Burke and David Nicholls all have plenty to thank all-weather racing for, and all three seem to have the potential to enter the higher levels of training given time. Often horses trained by these three can be available at long odds, and just as regularly outperform the market's expectations. That is also true of Gay Kelleway, in-house nowadays at Lingfield, and Mark Polglase who has his operation based at Southwell.

These stables' horses naturally have the benefit of being trained on the respective surfaces on which they race. Horses in these stables, that have been moved from other conventional training yards, are interesting to watch in the market on early outings.

A Curley footnote

Of all the punters in British and Irish racing over the years, none has been more difficult to read than Barney Curley. Nowadays a trainer at Newmarket, where news of the well-being or otherwise of his small string is kept closer than a dead-heat, Barney has enjoyed courting controversy throughout his various careers.

After his Magic Combination had won the Imperial Cup in March 2000, a handicap hurdle sponsored by bookmaker Sunderlands, the trainer refused to accept a trophy from the sponsors. He blamed the racing authorities for not sorting out the problem of punters like himself not being able to get their money on when they want to.

When I try to assess a race in which Barney Curley has a runner, I usually expect him to win it. If I back his horse it invariably runs a bad race, but just as often it gets up to stuff one I have backed.

The bookmakers have a built-in antenna that enables them to anticipate a possible 'touch'. However, Barney's runners are relatively few and far between, and no bookmaker can feel qualified to judge their chances, not simply because they run infrequently, but because the evidence for them one way or the other is never compelling. Magic Combination, for example, looked an improving sort the previous winter, but a single run in the season leading up to his Sandown win ended with a P (pulled up) on his record. Mean-minded and over-cautious the bookmakers may well sometimes be, but sitting ducks at a range where Barney is the man holding the rifle they are not.

CHAPTER FIVE

The Racing Year

Britain has 59 licensed racetracks, compared with France's 260. But whereas in France only a handful attract interest beyond a purely local stage, in Britain the sport is nationally represented by all the racecourses.

How British racing compares

In Britain, there is a division between Flat racing on the turf from late March to early November (with a sprinkling of all-weather racing all year), and National Hunt jumping. Apart from on the busiest Bank Holidays, all the racing is televised in betting shops and most meetings are covered live by the Racing Channel each day. Punters in the betting shops scan the papers and seek out winners anywhere from Ascot to Sedgefield, Newmarket to Market Rasen. The easy winner of a selling hurdle race at even money is of equal use to the punter who finds it, as the winner of the Derby who comes in at the same price. These tracks can be right-handed or left-handed, sharp or stiff, undulating or flat, with short straights or long run-ins.

In contrast, in France many racecourses operate with a single festival meeting, usually on a summer Sunday. These programmes will often include Flat, Anglo-Arab, hurdle and steeplechase races, intermingled with trotting – which still has an equal importance with its thoroughbred counterpart in that country, both in terms of public interest and betting activity.

The prime thoroughbred racing centres on Longchamp, which hosts the spring and autumn Classic races as well as the big Prix de l'Arc de Triomphe meeting. The 'Arc', Europe's most important all-aged championship race over a mile and a half, is the centrepiece of a two-day card which is festooned with major events for horses of either sex and in all age groups, including the two-year-olds.

Chantilly, the major French training centre about 25 miles north of central Paris, takes over as the focus of interest in early summer. The equivalent races to the Epsom Derby and Oaks are featured on this charming course which has a big chateau on the far side from its old-fashioned, small grandstands.

Longchamp takes over again at the end of June, before the whole of the Parisian racing scene, including its administration, decamps to the Normandy coast for the ever-expanding Deauville season. Late July and the whole of August are spent at this fashionable resort where the racing shares the limelight with the beaches, shops, smart hotels, golf, polo and the neighbouring Trouville casino for the leisure franc.

All year, French jump racing is centred on Auteuil, a beautiful track, like Longchamp in the middle of the Bois de Boulogne, with a mid-summer climax for the Grand Steeple Chase.

Americans, in another contrast, have grown up with a system of dirt racing which is conducted for the most part on tight circuits, universally left-handed, of a mile in circumference or thereabouts. The turf tracks are usually set inside what they term the Main Track, and at places like Gulfstream Park, home of the 1999 Breeders' Cup meeting, the turf course is no longer than seven furlongs for once round.

Three North American courses, which do at least offer a little variety from this unremitting uniformity, are Belmont Park in New York, Santa Anita in Los Angeles, and Woodbine, Canada's premier track in Toronto. Belmont, almost a mile and a half round, is a spectacular venue where 80,000 or more can fill the grandstand and pay just a few dollars for a seat on Belmont Cup day, when the final leg of the Classic Triple Crown is staged. I think Belmont is my favourite out of these, although the beautifully designed Arlington Park in Chicago runs it close. Santa Anita's uniqueness in the USA is its down-hill turf course of six and a half furlongs, which joins the turf oval entering the straight and has been a suitable stage for many equine acquisitions from Europe over the years.

Keeneland in Lexington, Kentucky, is a venue best known for its annual bloodstock sales, particularly those each July and September when some of the world's best-bred and most eagerly sought yearlings are offered for sale. But Keeneland also hosts two important racing meetings in the spring and autumn. The dirt track, as at

Santa Anita, is routinely conventional, but the feature is a European-style grass track. This has been given a small upward and downward gradient along the backstretch, which also has a kink off to the right, to add some modicum of interest.

That apart, the regular fare at the US courses, especially at the minor tracks, is a series of claiming races, mostly over six furlongs or a mile, with 'ordinary' prize money. The best courses, on the other hand, offer fantastic money. These are the tracks which envious British owners and trainers cite to illustrate their claim for much better prizes at home, without acknowledging the larger proportion of cheap claiming races held elsewhere.

Another big difference between American and British racing is that most US horses are stabled and trained at the tracks where they run. These horses are housed in barns on what is termed 'the Backstretch', and the activity on the track every morning is worth a visit.

A month-by-month account

For a racing professional the time of year often directs one's feet towards certain tracks. In a normal year I would probably visit about 40 of the 59 and would expect to visit the majority of the remainder every two or three years.

January
The snag here is that the days are so short. Any severely cold night means that frost probably will not be out

of the ground in time for the scheduled early starts, although recent years have been relatively problem-free.

Among the smaller tracks, Folkestone – where improvements have been steady under Arena Leisure's ownership – is an easy run for me down the M20 (as long as the M25 is kind). Sometimes a high-class horse finds its way to Folkestone, as was the case with Rough Quest who won a novice hurdle there in the same season he won his Grand National at Aintree.

Another easy run, this time up the M1, is to Towcester, a track which offers a much more testing aspect than Folkestone. Both are right-handed, but while speedy types can win around Folkestone, at Towcester stamina is the main requirement. The long back straight is merely the aperitif to the final arduous climb, with a hill to stop even apparently unassailable leads.

Hugo Bevan, who has been a skilful course clerk at Towcester for many years, also handles the track at Huntingdon, straight up the A1 from London. Huntingdon, perfectly flat, is a compromise between Folkestone and Towcester, and also plays host to some decent performers through the winter season, especially young hurdlers.

Often, in tough winters, Ascot's abandonments have enabled me to make an early call at Warwick, which would be a wonderful viewing track from the stands but for a massive hill behind the winning post which blocks out three or four fences.

The Victor Chandler Chase, which has its permanent home at Ascot, was switched to Warwick a few years ago and the race was equally satisfactory, despite being staged on a left-handed as opposed to right-handed track.

There is a long-distance chase at a later January meeting which always generates plenty of interest. In 2000, it took on extra significance, in its new persona as the Tote Scoop6 Handicap Chase, as the vehicle for the bonus race with a fund exceeding £1 million. One group of punters were the single winners of the Scoop6 win pool the previous week. Unsurprisingly, they failed to nominate the 20-1 winner Choisty, making a seasonal reappearance.

Intrepid travellers wishing to avoid weather problems in mid-winter have a serious option to travel north during the month to Musselburgh. A walk-on ticket at Heathrow to Edinburgh and a six-mile taxi ride to the coast offers an interesting afternoon on the nearest to an all-weather surface on any turf track. Races are run at a fast pace, and regular course winners are plentiful. I paid my first visit there many years ago to watch a horse in which I had an interest run on the Flat. The then veteran jockey John Seagrave, later a greyhound trainer, was unseated and landed smack bang on his crash helmet. He got back on what proved an unwilling partner and the result was predictably dire.

January is also the signal for the gearing-up of action on the all-weather tracks. Arena Leisure now own all three – Lingfield, Southwell and Wolverhampton – and the period of greatest intensity is the nine weeks from the start of the year. During this period, Arena have a fixture on every day at one or other track, and in some instances at two of them on those Saturdays when Wolverhampton is scheduled for an evening meeting.

The differing surfaces at the three tracks mean that

form does not translate necessarily from one to the others. There is a tendency for the two Midlands tracks to be more uniform in terms of results. Both tracks have a sand surface known as Fibresand, which is much deeper than that at Lingfield, which is known as Equitrack. A rule of thumb is that Lingfield suits fast-ground turf performers, and soft-going horses tend to do best at Southwell, which is deeper than Wolverhampton.

Over the years the quality of the horses contesting races at the three tracks has improved, and fewer of the apparently endless six-furlong sellers and claimers are included. The decision to raise rating bands and divide handicaps rather than sellers has improved the overall standard.

Running Stag, a horse good enough to win valuable races in the USA against their high-class turf performers, was an unsuccessful Lingfield visitor late in 1999, yet proved good enough to give a close race to top international performer Jim and Tonic in Hong Kong later in that winter. In January and February, Zanay won three races in a row at Lingfield and showed himself to be approaching the Running Stag class when winning a fourth, the winter Derby, in March.

Zanay's exploits were reward for his two owners, who over the years have played a big part in the career of the trainer Jacqui Doyle. Tom Ford, one of the two, had approached me a long time earlier to recommend a stable in the Home Counties. In those days Jacqui was based with her ex-husband in Hertfordshire, and Tom took up my recommendation. Unlike me, wasting my time in newspapers, Tom did a proper job as a City broker and

122 • Pocket Racing Guide

was able to retire when still young and fit enough to enjoy his money.

Trainers such as David Nicholls and David Chapman have proved adept at rekindling the enthusiasm of other stables' cast-offs and winning sequences of races on the sand surfaces. Indeed, Nicholls' wins in this sphere were the springboard for his own much more publicised achievements in recent turf seasons, especially with sprinters.

Many racing journalists would rather watch paint dry than go to the all-weather action, but the people who count are voting with their feet. Winners are there to be backed, and because the horses run regularly the form tends to be easier to interpret than for jumping at the same stage of the season. I like the informality of these meetings and the catering at all three is acceptable and excellent value.

February

Although I have yet to reach as far north as Kelso, every year I do look forward to its early February fixture which follows soon after the same track's late January date which has the Morebattle Hurdle as its centrepiece. This card is equally appealing and offers variety. Kelso is another of those tracks with a testing finish designed to halt the non-stayer. Over the years, many specialists have farmed races there.

The North West is not too well catered for by racetracks. Chester is confined to Flat racing, and the little-used Aintree course has not staged any Flat racing for around 25 years. Happily, Haydock Park offers decent class racing under both codes and its location, right on the M6 and halfway between Liverpool and Manchester along the East Lancs Road, ensures excellent crowds. The late February fixture, which features the De Vere Gold Cup (formerly the Greenalls Gold Cup) is a significant Grand National trial. I always enjoy Haydock, whose late May Saturday Flat card is also attractive.

While the North and Scotland can be susceptible to the weather at this time of year, the West Country often escapes in even harsh winters. Taunton provides low-class racing for the most part, but usually offers a Martin Pipe or Paul Nicholls winner. The sharp track is often compensated by softish ground in February and the pace of the races means that stamina does come into play. Wincanton, Taunton's nearest neighbour to the east, does attract a higher class of animal, and its late February card includes potential Cheltenham festival runners. The Jim Ford Gold Cup attracts Tote Gold Cup contenders, while Champion Hurdle aspirants can be found in the Kingwell Hurdle line-up. This race was won by Alderbrook on his way to Cheltenham success during the 1990s.

March

This month represents the beginning of the turn of the seasons, not just climatically, but also where racing is concerned. March means Cheltenham, but just a week later there is the start of Flat turf racing at Doncaster, where the Lincoln Handicap is the feature.

In between those two events, a couple of jumping fixtures have at one time or another benefited from their proximity to the Cheltenham Festival. Fakenham, in the middle of nowhere – or more precisely in deepest East Anglia – is a tiny sharp circuit, but it tends to be chosen to be the vehicle for any Tote Jackpot carry-overs from Cheltenham, which ends the previous day. The racing is modest and the trick is to identify the horse that will adapt to the track. Big boats should be left alone, and the handy types are the ones to back. The next day, at Uttoxeter, those Irishmen who have spent an extra day in their hotels like to finish off their English holiday with an afternoon at this superbly run Staffordshire track.

The highlight of this fixture is the Midlands Grand National, a four-miles-and-a-quarter marathon, which also tends to include a few Irish horses, either adding a second run to their Cheltenham exertions, or more likely on a shrewdly planned raid. Tony Martin is a trainer to watch out for on these occasions.

A week later the Flat is quickly into its stride. Catterick, in North Yorkshire, stages a card in the second week of the Flat. It is often possible to find a winner or two with horses fit either from jumping or the all-weather. Also, two-year-olds that have run with some promise at Doncaster the previous week often manage to beat well-backed newcomers at Catterick, because of their racetrack experience.

April
Several other northern tracks get going on the Flat during this month, but a bigger target for trainers in the south, notably Kim Bailey, is the jumping card at Perth. This right-handed circuit has a character of its own, and as the

northernmost track in Britain it requires a fluid timetable – no chance of an away day here.

On the Flat, three Yorkshire courses are magnets for Newmarket trainers. In his Newmarket days, you could always back John Gosden to win the three-year-old maiden at Ripon, one of the nicest tracks in the country. Set close to the A1 and just a few hundred yards from the beautiful Fountains Abbey, Ripon offers a good test and some decent-class racing through the year.

Thirsk is situated to the south-east of Ripon and is a left-handed track. I like the mile-and-a-half three-year-old maiden. Usually a stayer from the Maktoum string wins this and later in the year will normally be targeting the Queen's Vase at Royal Ascot. I must confess, however, that my preference is for Beverley, my lucky track as owner and punter over the years.

The first horse to run in my colours won there many years ago. In 1999, Hi-Jenny – claimed from Hors La Loi III's owner Paul Green for just 2000 guineas at Folkestone the previous year – won a handicap there first time out. Unfortunately I was otherwise occupied at Newmarket's Craven meeting, but the bookies paid out. When David Loder was establishing his Newmarket stables in the 1990s, I pointed out that the type of races Beverley habitually staged seemed to be suitable for a number of his horses. Over the next few years, David – a brilliant trainer and good friend – won a string of races and at an average exceeding 60 percent.

May

I look forward every year to the first week of May and racing at Chester. The 2000 and 1000 Guineas are over. The hectic May Bank Holiday is past and now it's three days at the wonderfully intimate but busy Chester racetrack. Unless the weather is unkind, you can bet that the grass will be immaculate, the fashions will be well up to York's August standard, and the racing will be informative. It was at Chester in 1999 that I saw enough in Oath's impressive Dee Stakes victory to anticipate victory for him at Epsom. In the winner's circle moments after the race, I remember receiving calls from owner Prince Ahmed bin Salman and the Thoroughbred Corporation Manager Dick Mulhall, respectively from Riyadh and Los Angeles. I told them both I thought he'd win at Epsom. It was a relief to be right for once.

Chester's big race is the Chester Cup, run over two complete circuits and a bit more of the dead flat, almost circular course, which lies within the old city walls and alongside the River Dee. Massive crowds are normal, not just for this fixture, but for the summer evening programmes in July. The Cup is sometimes won by a fit, high-class hurdler, perhaps one that has improved through the winter.

Maiden races at Nottingham can throw up a smart performer, and Newmarket-based Henry Cecil often chooses the Midlands track for debut runs by some of his better horses. In recent seasons, Nottingham's Executive has decided to stop racing over jumps, so now all its fixtures are on the Flat. The luxury for Nottingham is that the old hurdles track now doubles as an auxiliary Flat race track and the ground is usually very well maintained and rarely suffers from too much wear.

Jumping continues in the North. I still recall with some affection and rather more disbelief that, in the aftermath of Lester Piggott's 2000 Guineas win on Rodrigo de Triano, I chose to drive the 300 miles to Northumberland for a Saturday night Hexham fixture. Needless to say, I saw the last two races, and probably exceeded the permitted 70 mph for at least some of the way. The track is not exactly memorable, but it provided the scene for a long-ago coup when Santopadre won a selling hurdle in the last stride for my pal Wilf Storey's local stable.

Another less than wise cross-country double-header in May, from Chester to a Sedgefield night meeting, did produce a well-merited speeding ticket. On the map, Chester and Sedgefield do not look that far away, but I'd already travelled almost 200 miles when a traffic policeman stopped me as I accelerated down a sudden descent on the trans-Pennine route. Having been stuck behind a slow truck for five miles before the abrupt sign for a dual carriageway, I thought the relief at the prospect of a clear road was understandable. 'We catch a lot of people here,' smiled the nice policeman. I've not been back that way since.

Cartmel comes along but a couple of times a year, but the three days in late May – Saturday, Bank Holiday Monday and Wednesday – give the Lakeland track a little national exposure. Again, attendances are invariably large, and the quirky finishing straight – which bisects the rest of the course and takes the horses behind many spectators to the finish – gives the track its own appeal.

June

If you like rhododendrons, go to Newcastle in late June. The normal way into the Gosforth Park track is along a narrow road adjacent to the local hotel of the same name, and each side is festooned with the mauve blooms. The racing is not bad either. Plenty of Stan Clarke's famous green paint has transformed the look of what was a neglected dump for many years, and a trip for Friday night at the races, an overnight stay in the Gosforth Park, and then the Northumberland Plate meeting on the Saturday makes for an enjoyable weekend.

The 'Plate', a two-mile handicap which can attract horses that are just below group-race class, carries a big prize nowadays. Martin Pipe likes to challenge for this stayers' prize, which he won in 1999 with Far Cry.

Mid-June offers the longest days of the year, and the intimate Hamilton Park course, a few miles from Glasgow, runs two night fixtures. Hamilton is similar in layout to Salisbury, with a loop rather than a circuit, enabling races to be run up to an extended mile and five furlongs. Horses can build impressive records there, and Scottish trainer Linda Perratt often comes up with a winner at big odds.

Few fixture clashes during 1999 made less sense than the doubling up of Newcastle with its close neighbour Carlisle on the opening day of Newcastle's three-day Plate meeting. The same clash was scheduled for 2000, which suggested neither track minded much. Carlisle's sensible course management offered generous prize money for their historic Cumberland Plate and were rewarded for a low-rating race with a big, competitive field. I enjoy

Carlisle, especially in the summer. It gets a bit raw during the jumps season and the uphill finish reinforces the feeling of spartan rigour.

Windsor, by contrast, is dead flat and winds in a figure of eight to accommodate the twists of the River Thames near Windsor Castle. Now under the Arena banner, Windsor is the regular Monday night venue for West London race fans. The regular improvements made by the previous management in recent years have cemented the track's special place in racing. Crowds are strong and the racing itself is always competitive, with plenty of runners being the norm all through the season.

July

One of the major tracks, Sandown Park, does not have a recognised festival fixture. Indeed, all Sandown's meetings are of either one or two days' duration. The July meeting features the Coral–Eclipse Stakes, a Group 1 test over ten furlongs for three-year-olds and upwards. That is a major summer highlight and second only to its late-April mixed Flat/NH meeting. The weather is invariably sunny on this July weekend and the 'Eclipse' figures high in my list of racing memories.

The year was 1969 and Park Top, the hot favourite, was beaten by Wolver Hollow. I watched the race at home on television and then rushed off to my first and only wedding, timed unusually it now seems for 4 o'clock. The church was just five minutes at full gallop from the house. Owing to Sandown's facility for late starts, the best man and myself arrived after the bride had made two circuits in her expensive car. For me, the good thing about the 'Eclipse', a race I find as difficult as many Sandown races to predict, is that it serves to remind me to buy an anniversary present after all these years.

Some of the wettest days I have ever spent on racecourses were at Salisbury in the 1980s. Nowadays, it is usually sunny when I go there, and on a hot day there is no feeling of haste at Salisbury, which attracts a solid local audience from Wiltshire and its surrounds. Many of the old stand-bys of Salisbury have retired, but Ian Balding, Richard Hannon and Mick Channon usually clock up a few winners each year.

July enables Pontefract to make the latest afternoon starts in the business – no doubt the locals have to stay late to finish up making the cakes. The amazing track encloses much of a local park and a full circuit is comfortably above two miles. Apart from the Queen Alexandra Stakes at Royal Ascot, Pontefract offers the longest Flat race in the calendar, over two miles and five furlongs. With a full seven-furlong rise from the bottom of the hill, this ranks as an extreme stamina test and it is usually won by a wide margin.

The seaside season is in full swing by now, and one trip I never mind making is out to the east coast and Yarmouth. Surprise results are not unusual there, and when the ground gets firm, as it often does at this time of the year, it is safer to back the specialist trainers in the frequent apprentice races. Michael Bell does especially well in this category. Yarmouth has an amazing fish shop on the way out back to the road to Norwich, right on the path from the track. Whatever time you leave Yarmouth, the shop is always not quite open.

Market Rasen is a pleasant track in Lincolnshire and a visit can be combined with a look at Lincoln Cathedral. The racing is enjoyable and Charlie Moore is a hard-working boss there. (Charlie went to the same school as my son, so I try to be nice to him.) The track is right-handed and the races are truly run. Although the ground can be soft, speed horses usually have an advantage in the summer, and it seems that form works out pretty well.

August

In the old days (i.e. 1995), Newton Abbot and Market Rasen shared the opening of the new jumps season after a full two-month break. Nowadays, jumping never stops – even though for accounting purposes it is split into two parts. Summer breaks in the West Country can thus be combined with some August racing; and if the quality is dubious, the chance of winning a few bob to defray expenses is good. Martin Pipe and Tony McCoy will no doubt continue their usual ravenous summer pastime, so that three and four wins daily apiece is always possible. Newton Abbot requires a handy, pacy horse, notably in summer, but naturally under such conditions accurate jumping is vital.

There is a holiday bias at Brighton, too, with more Clarke-inspired green paint, and in this case a multimillion pound improvements scheme in the first year since he took charge. Brighton has had a somewhat raffish image ever since Graham Green's *Brighton Rock* was translated into a film with Richard Attenborough in the lead role as Pinky, the young hoodlum. The gangs are no longer visible, but the healthy breezes still occasionally turn nasty into a sea fret, which obscures the entire course. Racing is of a modest level, but the August fixture is sadly no more. It was once part of a long Sussex season, which included Goodwood in the preceding week and the long-closed Lewes.

Considering it can be hidden under several feet of water in wet winters, the track at Worcester provides jump racing for much of the year. Wisely, the course has opted for a spring-to-summer schedule, with three of the fixtures (two evening) coming in August. The ground always has sufficient moisture from the adjacent River Severn to attract runners in the summer, and this is the best option for mid-year jump racing in the country. The fields are often big, but the track is not testing and speed horses do well.

September

Twice each year, Ayr comes to the forefront of British racing, each time in opposition, in television terms, with equally strong programmes at Newbury. That it should be these two tracks which always clash is a coincidence, as a couple of years ago the courses' respective clerks of the course, Mark Kershaw (Ayr) and Richard Pridham (Newbury), effected a transfer deal. Pridham inherited a course where financial affairs had not always flowed smoothly. A polite, hard-working man, Pridham continued Kershaw's good work and the track's fortunes remain in the ascendant.

The Scottish National meeting in April is quite a favourite, but it is the six-furlong Ayr Gold Cup in mid-

September which appeals most. Sunny weather, massive fields and the chance of some big-priced winners bring in the crowds, and the racing is highly competitive.

It is more low-key at Fontwell, but this course is close enough to the Sussex coast at Bognor Regis for late holiday-makers to stop off for an afternoon. The chase course at Fontwell is a figure of eight, and the only one such now that Windsor is no longer a jumps track. The hurdlers travel around the outside and it takes two circuits for the two and a quarter miles to be completed. An uphill run-in, taken in all three times in hurdles of the minimum trip, makes an element of stamina important.

Bath, like Brighton, is another track where the weather can make sudden alterations. The Bath track at Lansdowne is high above the city and can be very rugged on a bad day and baking on a hot one. By September the extremes are less frequent, and the regular sprints around the sharp track, with its false straight before the actual short run-in, often go to course specialists.

October

It does not befall many racing officials to originate an idea that offers improved opportunities for smaller racehorse owners, so Lord Zetland's far-sighted Redcar Gold Trophy – based on a stallion's median sales figures of his progeny at auction – rates as a worthy and successful invention. Median races have developed into a serious secondary level of maidens, especially for two-year-olds, so the top-class sales buys from Newmarket's Houghton and Keeneland in Kentucky are kept out of the way.

Redcar offers good racing all year, but in an area where racecourse attendance is never going to be widespread it will remain a smaller track.

Court proceedings concerning the ownership of Sedgefield racecourse have offended some observers, especially the locals, but it seems inevitable that Stan Clarke will soon add it to his portfolio. This Co Durham course is another minor track, but it does draw big crowds, particularly for the night meetings when the cars park all round the main buildings. In some recent seasons there has been less grass than mud on the track, but that situation seems to have improved greatly. The racing remains modest but competitive.

Stratford-on-Avon's big day comes in late May when the top young hunters meet, usually including a future star of hunter chasing, and in the case of Teeton Mill a top performer under Rules. The October date comes as a welcome diversion from the less interesting Flat racing of a minor kind at that late stage of the season. Stratford is sharp and the races always truly run. You need a handy animal, and my last visit revealed Heart as a hurdler to follow. She has justified that status since.

The end of October signals the North's first decent meeting at Wetherby. In 1999, the Charlie Hall Chase at that fixture featured not just See More Business, the reigning Gold Cup winner, but also Looks Like Trouble, who, at Cheltenham in March 2000, took his crown. Throughout the winter Wetherby offers top-class racing, with an emphasis on good chases. Apart from the 'Charlie Hall', there are the Rowland Meyrick and Castleford Chases at the two-day Christmas meeting. There are few fairer tracks than Wetherby, and in chases the fences take plenty of jumping.

November

An early November date for the William Hill Haldon Gold Cup, the best race run all season at Exeter, means that anyone visiting the Breeders' Cup in the United States might not be able to take the trip down to the West Country. Most years that would be a misfortune. In 1999 it was a genuine shame, as the highly impressive young chaser Flagship Uberalles proved he was the two-mile chaser of the future when beating a field including Direct Route and Edredon Bleu. At that stage only five years old, Flagship Uberalles was resuming where he had left off in the Arkle Chase at Cheltenham the previous March. Exeter is situated within a wooded area just outside the city, and the two-mile circuit is one of the largest in the country. Normal fare is of a lower level, but generally racing at Exeter is competitive.

Hereford is one of the smaller tracks. Fairly flat, right-handed and with a short finishing straight, it requires a handy horse to win there. The fences are not formidable and the racing is middle rank at best. Occasionally, a decent novice hurdler or chaser is given a relatively undemanding early assignment at Hereford.

Neither Hereford nor Exeter stages Flat racing. Leicester does from April until October, but then switches to jumping for the winter. In November, fields for the hurdle races in particular can be large and many trainers like Leicester as it provides a good test of jumping.

The biggest race of the month, though, is clearly

Newbury's Hennessy Cognac Gold Cup, a race which often sets up an improving horse for a programme with the Cheltenham Gold Cup the following March as its logical outcome. Newbury, which also runs important meetings over both codes throughout the year, is one of the fairest courses with only slight undulations. It is wide and galloping in nature. Apart from the 'Hennessy', the Tote Gold Trophy in February and the new Aon Chase at the same meeting are major jump races. On the Flat, the Greenham Stakes in April is a trial for the 2000 Guineas.

One of my earliest racing memories was seeing the great Peter (now Sir Peter) O'Sullevan back a 7-1 Ian Balding-trained winner at Newbury in 1964 the day before I took my Economics A-level examination. Sir Peter's *Daily Express* tip had nominated a different horse, which I, as an O'Sullevan fan, had backed. It came nowhere, having started favourite. I didn't know they were allowed to do that!

December

You get some very soft ground at Bangor-on-Dee, a little track just inside Wales. Under the conditions which prevail in the winter, Bangor takes plenty of getting, and horses are often strung out after chases.

One day I was planning to go to the course, and my great friend Richard Kent, who runs Helshaw Grange Farm in Shropshire, invited me to have lunch in the box. I didn't make it that day, and sadly still haven't. Richard kindly told me later that, far from his having a box, in fact there is not even a proper grandstand, but a mound from which people watch the races.

It rarely gets quite so muddy at Ludlow, and despite there being four fences in the home straight, this is not such a stamina test. My earliest recollection about Ludlow concerns a race thirty years ago when a horse called Bermondsey won. The horse's owner, a comedian called Des O'Connor (whatever happened to him?), happily agreed to an impromptu interview and I can still remember his stylish leather jacket. Nice bloke, and he still has a horse in training, too.

By now the days are running out and getting shorter, with Christmas and the Boxing Day bonanza to come. All that's left, remembering the early starts and finishes, is a quick dash down to Plumpton. If the visibility worsens, the horses never get very far away, but strangely for a short track of around a mile they often get very tired. In the old days a lot of the top jockeys, including Fred Winter, hated riding at Plumpton, which has a 'trap' fence at the start of the downhill run on the far side. I quite like the atmosphere at Plumpton; and when Peter Savill, a major shareholder in the course, has a runner there trained in far-off Yorkshire by Mrs Reveley, that clearly spells a chance for him and us to get some Christmas money. See you in the New Year!

British racing: A success story

Despite all the complaints about the unfairness of the funding system of British racing, there is no doubt that improvements in the amount of money filtering down under the established order have been significant. Prize money has been increasing steadily and attendances have been similarly buoyant.

The fact is that British racing remains a sport where the public generally feels for the horses as individual personalities. In the USA, on the other hand, the bread-and-butter racing is very much a numbers game, and to an extent that is true also of French racing. There are exceptions of course: cases like Cigar, or in 1999 Charismatic, who came from lowly company to win the Kentucky Derby and the Travers before just failing to complete a Triple Crown clean-sweep when breaking down in the Belmont Stakes.

The big British racing festivals – Royal Ascot, Cheltenham and Aintree, as well as Glorious Goodwood and the streamlined Derby meeting – have never been more popular. Indeed Royal Ascot and Cheltenham have had to restrict crowds on some of the days, which have become all-ticket with the sold-out notices appearing weeks before the event.

Kempton on Boxing Day

There is an immense contrast between the day-to-day diet of racing and the quickening of interest which accompanies the various big meetings through the year. Kempton at Christmas is best considered as the first of these, although it inhabits the previous calendar year. The King George VI Chase, currently sponsored by George Ward of Tripleprint and Doubleprint fame, is the most important race of the first half of the jumps season proper, which nowadays runs from August to late April. The 'King George', a steeplechase run over three miles, is a test of stamina and speed when the ground is fast, but the pace at which races are habitually run there makes it much more of a test with soft ground.

Some of my most exciting National Hunt days have been spent at Kempton, and I still remember the amazing performance of Captain Christy, beating the brilliant Bula, one of the great champions of the 1970s, by 30 lengths in a King George. More recently, the 1999 Cheltenham Gold Cup winner See More Business slaughtered a top class field in the final days of the old millennium to prove himself one of the outstanding steeplechasers of the decade.

Cheltenham in the spring

Kempton's Christmas meeting is of minor proportions, owing its status mostly to its timing, as seasonal revellers look for almost any respite from turkey and plum pudding. The next point on the calendar, however, is a festival with a capital F.

Whatever the accident of geomorphology, which scraped a bowl out of a part of the western Cotswold Hills and left the natural amphitheatre of Prestbury Park, it provided the ideal venue for high-class jumps racing. Inclines and descents, with testing fences added, combine with the meeting of the best chasers and hurdlers in Britain and Ireland, with an occasional French invader, to settle most of the arguments about the various championship contenders.

The Cheltenham Gold Cup, currently sponsored by the Tote, and the Champion Hurdle backed by the Irish paper group Jefferson Smurfit, rightly take centre stage, and the severity of each event can be gauged by the paucity of multiple winners, especially in recent times.

In the Gold Cup, run over three and a quarter miles, Irish-trained and American-owned L'Escargot was the last horse to win back-to-back renewals, 1970 and 1971. That achievement followed Arkle's hat-trick between 1964 and 1966. In 1998, See More Business might have matched L'Escargot but for being carried out by a horse pulling up, having started favourite. See More Business, trained in Somerset by the talented Paul Nicholls, made amends with victory when starting pretty much unfancied the following year.

In 2000 he started favourite in an epic contest marred by the death of the novice Gloria Victis, who fell two fences from home. See More Business faded into fourth behind new champion Looks Like Trouble.

Istabraq, Ireland's best hurdler of the modern era, ended a sequence of ten different winners when completing a Champion Hurdle double in 1999. The following year Istabraq equalled the hat-trick of the previous multiple winner, See You Then, whose triple ran from 1985-1987.

The Queen Mother Champion Chase, also over two miles, and the Bonusprint Stayers Hurdle, over three miles and a furlong, offer alternative opportunities for the best of the experienced horses that do not meet the correct requirements of the fixture's pre-eminent events.

Apart from these senior championship races in the two disciplines, there are also championship events over varying distances for novice horses, both over hurdles and in steeplechases. These are supplemented throughout the three midweek days by a series of ultra-competitive handicap races.

One thing that sets Cheltenham apart, other than the quality of the participants, is the size of the fields. Several of the hurdle races are contested by 30 runners, and any trainer who can guide a horse through all the potential pitfalls to get safely to the track and win a race of this competitiveness deserves the highest praise.

A most notable aspect of the meeting is the preponderance of the Irish. Many of the horses are trained on that side of the Irish Sea and many of the home team's horses were bred in Ireland. But the biggest manifestation of things Irish is the number of visitors who throng the enclosures. For most of a week every March, the hotels, pubs and restaurants in the town and its surrounding areas are packed to capacity and dominated by animated Irish voices.

The betting ring emphasises that aspect, not least since the influx of Irish bookmakers on the rails and in the main enclosure pitches, who have paid large sums for seniority positions under revised pitch rules. Betting levels are higher than at any other meeting – illustrating the point that, while the bigger crowds at Royal Ascot include many people principally watching other people, at Cheltenham it is the horses that attract all the attention.

Much later in the year, in mid-November, the Irish are again deeply involved in what is effectively the true starting point for the embryo jumps 'season'. The Murphy's Gold Cup (formerly 'the Makeson'), on the second day of a three-day fixture, has been strengthened in recent years, and Irish runners are commonplace. The crowds have improved, too.

Aintree: the National meeting

While the tears are still drying after the triumphs and tragedies of Cheltenham, jumping's second major festival is staged at Aintree in Liverpool. Martell, the French brandy house, might not have seemed an obvious sponsor for a meeting in the North West of England, but the company's blanket support for the entire three days, with the Martell Grand National as its core, has been both sustained for many years and inspired in its application.

If Cheltenham has its natural stage, Aintree and the Grand National has a history dating back more than 150 years, with drama and heroism in equal measure. The components are remarkably simple. The National has lent itself to sensational televiewing. The race, over a total of four and a half miles, entails two circuits of an open triangular track, added on to a more conventional racecourse for its middle and concluding phases.

Over the years the once fearsome fences have been modified and are now generally regarded as fairly mundane, with the exception of three key obstacles. These are the third fence, a ditch; the still-feared Chair in front of the stands, which is jumped only once, and Becher's Brook, which is a drop fence. Jumped in solitary comfort, even these can seem routine, but once 40 horses line up at the start and aim at the first obstacle, 400 yards ahead, adrenaline – equine and human – takes charge. Often, one faller at the head of the charge can trigger a multiple mêlée. Half a dozen casualties here can set the pattern for the rest of the first circuit, when the pitfalls posed by riderless horses include bringing down rivals at the time they are preparing to jump.

Most years, one particular incident is remembered. Perhaps the most famous is the inexplicable collapse of the Queen Mother's Devon Loch, only yards from the winning post with the race at his mercy. Theories include the horse's frightened reaction to the incredible roar from a crowd willing a royal success. Whatever the merits of that opinion, the incident provided a handy boost to the eventual amazing success of Devon Loch's jockey, Dick Francis, who wrote a succession of best-selling novels all with a racing background.

The 'Foinavon year' in 1967 is another well-remembered race, when almost the entire field was blocked by a scrum at the twenty-third of the fences, leaving the unconsidered 100-1 outsider to go clear and win. There were two more recent fiascos in the 1990s: a double false-start, which produced a void race in 1993; and in 1997 an IRA bomb warning, actually a hoax, necessitated a complete course evacuation and a two-day delay in staging the race.

Happy events have also featured at Aintree. In the 1970s the local favourite, Red Rum, proved himself the ultimate National horse. He won three times and finished second twice in five consecutive years from 1973 to 1977. Red Rum was trained a few miles along the Lancashire coast on the sands at Southport by a used-car salesman, Don (Ginger) McCain.

Soon after that, Aldaniti was successful in 1981, partnered by Bob Champion. The jockey, who for most of the year leading up to the race was undergoing chemotherapy treatment for cancer, survived and went on to train from a small stable in Newmarket for more than a decade.

By the end of the 1990s, the once-dingy Aintree had been transformed, thanks principally to Martell. Much-improved facilities brought bigger attendances, the re-introduction of the November meeting, and an evening fixture in the spring. These developments have left Aintree in its soundest financial situation since the Second World War.

Newmarket: the Guineas meeting

Newmarket's status as the centre of British horseracing has not always seemed secure. Admittedly, as the principal training centre, with several thousand horses in numerous stables around the town, it had obvious importance. The problem was the perception that its main track, the Rowley Mile, was hardly worthy of the distinction as racing's Headquarters.

Ancient stands, apart from a small head-on building, were provided for viewing over a unique track with a one-mile-and-a-quarter straight and no circular track. Indeed, the Rowley Mile's Cesarewitch course, over which the second leg of the 'autumn double' is staged, is two and a quarter miles long, yet contains just a single right-hand bend at halfway. Viewing of that race each year had been confined to the television screen, but the building of the £16 million Millennium Grandstand – ready for the opening meeting in 2000 – improved that for some lucky racegoers. The new stand, rising to five stories, offers opportunities for viewing long-distance races, admittedly with a powerful set of binoculars.

The second meeting of the Newmarket season, usually straddling the end of April and beginning of May, is a three-day fixture with a double Classic offering on the second and third days. The 2000 Guineas, open to three-year-old colts and fillies, and its female-only counterpart race, the 1000 Guineas, recall ancient financial values and denominations, but the two races' winners will earn much more in present-day cash terms and command vast sums in the international marketplace.

Newmarket stages races only on the Flat, and more than 30 days' racing are shared each year between the Rowley Mile course and its summer replacement, the 'July' course. All the meetings in July and August are staged on the latter, among which the regular Friday night dates are highly popular. They attract big crowds, who have musical entertainment from well-known bands to add to their entertainment.

A feature of this summer season is a three-day fixture in early July, with the July Cup as its centrepiece. This highly-competitive Group 1 six-furlong sprint offers a key clue to the eventual identity of the season's European champion sprinter.

Newmarket also stages some major events in its autumn season back on the Rowley Mile. Champions Day, in mid-October, includes the Group 1 Champion Stakes, a 10-furlong event. In practice that is often over-shadowed by the Group 1 Dewhurst Stakes, the year's most important two-year-old event over seven furlongs, as well as the two-and-a-quarter mile Tote Cesarewitch handicap.

Two weeks before that, the Tote Cambridgeshire provides the first leg of the 'autumn double'. A nine-furlong handicap, it usually attracts a full field of 36, the same number as the Cesarewitch, and is a massive betting event.

Epsom: the Derby and Oaks

If Cheltenham or Newmarket could be deemed suitable stages for top horseracing, the undulating chalk downs of Epsom might be the object of rather differing opinion. Historical accident rather than analytical planning has led to the most important of the season's Classic races being staged on this track, whose cambers and undulations are far from ideal for a heavily-built and immature horse. The fact that it is precisely that type of horse which tends to contest the Vodafone Derby each June has led to some calls for a rethink about the race itself and the entire European programme of major races.

It takes a special type of three-year-old colt or filly to cope with the rigours of the mile-and-a-half race against the accepted leaders of the generation. Rewards, in terms of re-sale value, are immense. Many recent winners have shown little on the track afterwards, but an almost certain multimillion dollar price tag will hang on to any Derby winner, whatever the subsequent achievements, or otherwise, at stud.

The Oaks is the fillies-only counterpart race, and is run on the Friday, the first of the two-day fixture. Oaks winners have been plentiful for the Maktoum family in general and Sheikh Mohammed in particular. It must be a cause of great puzzlement to that owner that neither his own maroon and white colours, nor the royal blue of his Godolphin training operation, have yet adorned an Epsom Derby winner, whereas he has owned two Champion Hurdle winners, Kribensis and Royal Gait.

Ascot: jewels and champions

The quality of racing over four days at Royal Ascot each June is uniformly high. Crowds are enormous, and some imaginative pricing, which enables racegoers to enter the capacious Silver Ring enclosure for just £2, attracts a wide spectrum of people, with hundreds of coach parties, especially of women, for Ladies Day on Thursday.

But it is at the other end of the massive track, which can accommodate 70,000 plus, that the main action takes all the attention, in the Royal Enclosure. Morning dress for the men and imaginative and costly fashions for the women provide the backdrop to such top races as the Gold Cup, run over two and a half miles, and the St James's Palace and Coronation Stakes, each over one mile.

The Gold Cup is one of the nicest anachronisms in racing, with its extreme distance conflicting with most of the trends in international racing, in which speed and more speed is the absolute criterion. Ironically, perhaps, the high cash value of the race has helped it become a higher-class contest in recent years, and indeed much bigger fields are regularly achieved nowadays than in earlier times.

The St James's Palace Stakes, for colts, has become the early-season barometer of mile talent in Europe. It is timed so that contestants of the English, French and Irish 2000 Guineas races can meet at Ascot. Similarly, the best fillies from the English, French and Irish 1000 Guineas often lock horns in the Coronation Stakes.

Four two-year-old races offer early indications of potential star performers. It was at Royal Ascot in 1999 that Fasliyev first showed his great ability when winning the Coventry Stakes. Fasliyev ended the year unbeaten, but sadly suffered a winter injury and was retired to stand at Coolmore stud in 2000.

The handicaps are also a big feature during this week. The Royal Hunt Cup, Ascot Stakes, Bessborough Stakes and Wokingham Stakes all attract massive betting activity. Fields of 32 are normal for the Hunt Cup, which is run over the straight mile course.

Another highlight of the Ascot racing year comes in late July. The two-day 'Diamond meeting' brings the big summer showdown of the various classic generations in the King George VI and Queen Elizabeth Diamond Stakes, sponsored by the de Beers company. The 'King George' has a wonderful roll of honour in its 50-year history, and the brilliant grey stallion Daylami began his big challenge for his Horse of the Year accolade in 1999 by winning this mile-and-a-half highlight in unchallenged fashion. Daylami went on to win the Irish Champion Stakes at Leopardstown and ended a wonderful career in style in the Breeders' Cup Turf when he gained a third verdict over the formidable Royal Anthem during the year.

There is also a September festival meeting, staged over two days immediately before the first autumn meeting at Newmarket. The most important race at the September meeting is the Queen Elizabeth II Stakes, which is run over the same round mile as the two big mile races for three-year-olds in June – but this time, older milers are in the opposition. Consequently, this race frequently identifies the champion miler in Europe.

Glorious Goodwood

The period between Royal Ascot and Goodwood's big late-July/early-August five-day fixture is generally low-key while holidays take hold in Britain. Apart from the three days of the Newmarket July meeting, Sandown's Eclipse Stakes meeting and the King George event at Ascot, racing is of an ordinary level.

Goodwood, however, the most picturesque course in Britain, is a magnet for racing fans, who flock to the Sussex venue. Where formality is the emphasis at Royal Ascot, Goodwood fashions are informal with lightweight suits and panama hats de rigeur.

The Sussex Stakes, over a mile, is a high-class race, but in recent years it has not been the target of many eventual miling champions. The Vodafone Stewards Cup is a major handicap sprint on the Saturday, the final day of the meeting, while high-class two-year-olds are often introduced here by some of the leading stables.

The Gordon Stakes, over a mile and a half, brings some late-developing three-year-olds, who have not been at the top of their generation, into the year's argument. Nedawi, a dead-heater in the 1998 Gordon Stakes with Rabah, went on to win the St Leger later that year. That Gordon Stakes was not my happiest moment in racing, as

Hitman, a horse in whom I have a share, started favourite, but was just over a length behind the dead-heaters in third.

York in August

Goodwood can often provide a springboard for the more concentrated excellence of the three-day York August meeting three weeks later. The leading three-year-old stayers of either sex have major opportunities; colts in the Great Voltigeur Stakes and the Yorkshire Oaks for fillies. The Nunthorpe Stakes over five furlongs is one of the most important sprints of the year, but the undoubted highlight is the Juddmonte International, a Group 1 race run over ten and a half furlongs.

Over the years, the Juddmonte Stakes has had many impressive winners. Back in the 1970s the great Brigadier Gerard suffered one of his few reverses when beaten by the Derby winner Roberto, ridden by the Brazilian rider Braulio Baeza. The most impressive winner of the race in recent times was undoubtedly Royal Anthem. In 1999, the Thoroughbred Corporation-owned four-year-old, ridden by the American Gary Stevens and trained by Henry Cecil, won by eight lengths.

Two-year-old excellence is represented in the Gimcrack Stakes over six furlongs, and throughout the three days the knowledgeable Yorkshire crowd offers a stylish Northern version of racecourse fashion.

Doncaster: the St Leger meeting

The oldest Classic race in the calendar is the St Leger, and it is also the longest of the five contests that comprise the annual classic programme for three-year-olds. The meeting coincides with the turning of the leaves in early September and the shortening of the days.

Run over an extended mile and three-quarters, which is worth in stamina terms a good two miles on a less arduous, galloping track than Doncaster, the St Leger is tough on horses, and often provides a thrilling conclusion. The Great Voltigeur at York, run over one and a half miles, often offers a clue and its winners tend to turn up at Doncaster. In 1999, Ramruma, winner of the Yorkshire Oaks, was aimed at the St Leger, and this game filly – who had also won the Epsom and Irish Oaks earlier in the year – did everything bar win. In the end, she was just outlasted by the Godolphin runner Mutafaweq. The winner gave his all, too, and apparently dehydrated, lashed out for some time in the winner's enclosure.

The other supporting races include the Park Hill Stakes, for fillies, also over the St Leger distance, and a race which Ramruma would undoubtedly have won had she been aimed there instead.

CHAPTER SIX

The Owners

Godolphin and the Maktoums from Dubai

Throughout history, no country has been as closely identified with a single sporting activity in quite the way that Dubai and its ruling family, the Maktoums, has become famous on a world stage for its connection with horseracing.

In the late 1970s, the young Sheikh Mohammed bin Rashid al Maktoum, third son of the ruler of Dubai, one of the United Arab Emirates, decided to buy a horse to be trained in England. By the early 1980s the sheikh and his three brothers, Maktoum, Hamdan and Ahmed, had all entered the sport of racing on an international scale, and were soon instrumental in causing the biggest upheaval in the world bloodstock market.

Noting that the English owner, Robert Sangster, had enjoyed astonishing success with his acquisitions of yearlings from the Keeneland July horse sales in Lexington, Kentucky, they quickly turned their attentions to that market. Sheikh Mohammed was soon leading the field, paying 10.2 million dollars for a single horse, Snaafi

Dancer – who proved a flop, never even making it to the racetrack.

In an attempt to keep ahead, Sangster paid a world-record 13.1 million dollars for another eventual 'nonentity', Empire Glory. I witnessed many of these exciting sales in Kentucky, and while the market had an inevitable costly fallout, by 1999 the signs were that bloodstock was again almost back to those heady days.

In the meantime, Sangster's own position as a world leader in the business gently evaporated. That said, his ownership of the Manton estate – where around 50 of his horses are trained now by John Gosden – still makes him a premier league player if not a potential champion.

Dubai's influence, meanwhile, increased rather than diminished. Upon the death of Sheikh Rashid, Mohammed's elder brother Maktoum took over as ruler of Dubai. The second brother, Hamdan, eventually moved sideways to enable his younger sibling Mohammed to become Crown Prince in addition to his political role as Defence Minister for the UAE. Throughout the 1980s Mohammed's energies were concentrated on the Dalham Hall stud in Newmarket, where some of his best racehorses were retired as stallions. Many high-class mares were sent to them, and a major breeding programme was carried out.

Sheikh Mohammed has shown himself to be an acknowledged poet and is regarded as a philosopher. I gained an early insight into that element of the sheikh's personality while I conducted one of his first interviews with a British newspaper, for the *Daily Telegraph*. We were discussing his plans for the stud, and he said: 'To set up a proper breeding operation does not take four years, it will take 40.' Almost halfway down that time scale, Dalham Hall has undergone significant change, with the entire focus of the Maktoum operation in general, and Sheikh Mohammed's messianic direction of it in particular, shifting from Newmarket to his palace's backyard in Dubai.

Dubai's original wealth was based on its crucial position on the trading route through the Gulf of Arabia, and trading was the emirate's lifeblood. Then, in 1960, the discovery of an oilfield just offshore produced the revenue that was to fuel Dubai's great step forward. All the time, though, as the little state was developed with cost apparently being of secondary importance, awareness that the oil would run out one day was paramount.

Thus, a policy was put in place to turn Dubai into a first-rate holiday and tourist destination, one based on top-quality hotels and seaside resorts, and with shopping facilities to entice the most compulsive shopoholic. Golf courses of an international championship calibre were established, with annual tournaments allied to the European tour, while Dubai also became a stop on world tennis and other sporting itineraries.

Amid all the impressive infrastructure, the pearl in Dubai's development was its magnificent – yet in some ways modest – racecourse. The stands are pleasing on the eye but unostentatious, the principal feature of the development being the quality of the sand and turf tracks.

In the mid-1990s the Dubai Turf Club, under Sheikh Mohammed's guidance, developed the idea for a World

Cup, run in the spring and designed to attract the top horses from around the world. Prize money, set at four million dollars for its first running but increased to six million for 2000, set it above the highest-value individual prize in the Breeders' Cup series – the Classic – for which it is an early-season complement.

The quality of runners in the Dubai World Cup was immediately of the highest calibre, and that success encouraged Sheikh Mohammed to instigate a World Championship in 1999, which included top-class races around the world.

The first World Championship proved a triumph for the admirable grey Daylami, who was acquired from his breeder, His Highness the Aga Khan, after the horse had won the French 2000 Guineas. His brilliant 1999 campaign, after which he won the Horse of the Year accolade for Europe, included winning the Breeders' Cup Turf race at Gulfstream Park, Florida, as well as the King George VI and Queen Elizabeth II Diamond Stakes, the Coronation Cup and the Irish Champion Stakes. For the 2000 season Daylami went back to his original home at the Aga Khan's stud in Ireland. His story could never have happened but for the sheikh's dissatisfaction with what he perceived as the unsatisfactory level of success of the horses trained for him by some of the leading trainers in Britain.

At first tentatively, as with his initial entry to the sport 20 years earlier, Sheikh Mohammed began a process of winter conditioning of some horses in Dubai. After a much-publicised split with his senior Newmarket trainer Henry Cecil, the numbers concerned in the winter move to Dubai increased. By 1994, under the banner of 'Godolphin' and with the Dubaian Saeed bin Suroor as trainer, these horses were winning classics and other major races in Britain and all around the world.

While Sheikh Mohammed is most easily identified as the spirit behind Godolphin, Sheikhs Maktoum, Hamdan and Ahmed are all energetic partners. All four brothers retain their individual ownership elements, but Godolphin's aspirations are paramount.

Thus, in 1998, trainer David Loder was enticed from his base in Newmarket to operate from the recently acquired former Evry racecourse near Paris, to oversee the development of a stable comprised almost exclusively of two-year-olds. The success of that project will not be judged on the specific achievements of those embryonic talents as juveniles under Loder's care, but on how they progress in the later stages of their careers. It has been the brilliant organisation of Godolphin, under its manager Simon Crisford and trainer Saeed bin Suroor, each directed by Sheikh Mohammed, which has identified the potential for success in older horses.

Many things can go wrong in a classic campaign. Take the example of Dubai Millennium, an unbeaten horse when he tackled the 1999 Derby at Epsom. It was judged that he failed to stay the distance, but by the end of the season his achievements in mile races, especially when easily winning the Queen Elizabeth II Stakes at Ascot, more than compensated for that single lapse.

The Dubai World Cup – which Dubai Millennium won so impressively for Godolphin in 2000 – puts a world focus on to Dubai, and the approval rating by the

Americans, which was vital to the race's success, can be assessed by the continued targeting of the race by the top horses in that country.

A further development of the Godolphin operation were instituted early in 2000 when Eoin Harty was announced as the trainer for an operation, again for developing two-year-olds, in California, with Santa Anita in Los Angeles as its focus. Godolphin sent a number of three-year-olds to compete in the USA in 1999, with the aim of producing a Kentucky Derby winner. That proved beyond them that time round, but the target has been identified, and some of Sheikh Mohammed's more recent statements indicate that he will not be deflected from the objective – as was the case when the original Dubai training project was so dismissively received eight years earlier.

The sheikh has said: 'Every obstacle is a stepping stone to your success'; and 'Stride on and the world will make way for you'; and perhaps fittingly for a man who reckons that in the race of life there is no finishing line: 'One man's blinkers are another man's focus.' There's no problem of focus for this extraordinary man.

But never mind the philosophy. Sheikh Mohammed will be remembered as the man who most influenced the British racing industry, bringing considerable employment to stable and stud workers and helping to ensure that British racegoers would be able to enjoy seeing some of the best horses in the world competing in our country. The owner of such stars as Halling and triple-classic winner Oh So Sharp, Sheikh Mohammed is now busily building up the next generation to take charge of the horse empire after he is no longer able or willing to give it sufficient attention to do it justice.

His eldest son, Sheikh Rashid, already has impressive knowledge of horseracing, and like his father is a talented rider. The careful planning which has nurtured Godolphin will also characterise the increasing importance of Sheikh Rashid within the Godolphin organisation.

The Coolmore stud

When there is a world leader of serious stature in any activity, it is preferable that there be at least one other balancing power, not least to put the leader's position into focus. On a world racing scale, that balance is adequately and increasingly provided by the Coolmore Stud operation, run by John Magnier. He can call on the added financial muscle of a number of associates, the most easily identifiable of whom is Michael Tabor.

John Magnier comes from Irish farming stock and first came to prominence after his marriage to Susan O'Brien, daughter of the legendary Irish trainer Vincent O'Brien. While Vincent was building the racing reputation of the Ballydoyle stable throughout a long career, Magnier became a part-owner in Coolmore Stud in Co Tipperary, with his father-in-law and Robert Sangster, the main horse owner in O'Brien's stable at the time. When Vincent retired from training in the early 1990s, Magnier moved on to centre-stage, a process hastened by Sangster's increased commitment to the cost of running his Manton training centre in England.

Strangely, it was when the Vincent O'Brien role was taken by his namesake, the unrelated Aidan O'Brien, that Magnier's fortunes exploded. Already Coolmore had become easily the most important European stud operation, with stallions of the calibre of Sadler's Wells, the perennial European champion, and the late, lamented Caerleon. Aidan O'Brien, who was only in his mid-twenties when arriving at Ballydoyle, soon showed that all the promise he had already revealed since marrying Anne-Marie Crowley, daughter of Joe Crowley, and taking control of that family's established stable, was merely a hint of future greatness.

Aidan O'Brien took charge of the sales purchase Istabraq, bought for J. P. McManus by the Irish agent Timmy Hyde, and the horse showed himself to be the best hurdler for at least 30 years with a string of big race wins including multiple Champion Hurdles at Cheltenham.

At around the time Istabraq joined O'Brien, Magnier, McManus and other associates enjoyed considerable success in the world's money trading markets. Among the group was the former East End bookmaker Michael Tabor, who had recently sold his string of betting shops for £30 million. Tabor's stake quickly grew, and since the alliance with Magnier was cemented, Tabor – both in his own right and in partnership with Sue Magnier – has become one of the world's top three owners of racehorses.

The Coolmore–O'Brien link produced nine of the top 20 two-year-olds in the 1999 International Classification. They were headed by the unbeaten Fasliyev, who unfortunately had to be retired after sustaining an injury at the end of that year. Fasliyev, winner of the Coventry Stakes at Royal Ascot, was a typical O'Brien trainee, beautifully-bred yet capable of winning major races as a two-year-old. During the same year, Stravinsky gave the partners the distinction of a sprint championship, secured with a brilliant display in the Group 1 July Cup at Newmarket.

The knack of producing precocious horses with classic pedigrees means that Coolmore can operate at both ends of the stud market. If a breeder wants speed he has it in abundance. If he wants to produce a classic winner, there's Sadler's Wells – at a price. His fee was £125,000; but then Coolmore can point to the fact that, considering his achievements – the Derby apart – he is cheap compared with the top US stallion Storm Cat, whose 300,000 dollar fee translates to around £180,000. Needless to say, the ever-astute Magnier secured a batch of nominations to Storm Cat during 1999.

As with any organisation of merit, Coolmore has a powerful back-up team. Demmy O'Byrne is a respected vet who acts as Michael Tabor's personal advisor and agent. Timmy Hyde is another close colleague, while the talented Paul Shanahan handles much of the day-to-day activity and is Coolmore's main man at bloodstock sales time.

There is little doubt that the Coolmore organisation has done a lot to re-invent Ireland as a successful country. Its triumphs have mirrored the Irish nation's growth in confidence and prosperity. Its racing and breeding have always been important to Ireland, and the fact that in Coolmore they have the world's most successful and commercially viable horse business is a matter of great national pride.

As for Michael Tabor, it is sometimes hard to believe that this one-time bookmaker and avowed punter could re-invent himself in a short time to become such a prominent racehorse owner. In 1995, before his European adventure got into stride, he won the Kentucky Derby with Thunder Gulch, trained by D. Wayne Lukas, and has been a power on both sides of the Atlantic ever since.

To accompany his altered status within the industry, Tabor has also added a calm demeanour and a genuine modesty about his achievements. As a punter he knows that, like the value of any other investment, the value of bloodstock can go down as well as up. But then, it would need to go down a long way to make much difference to Mr Tabor.

Robert Sangster

Even before my first trip to Kentucky for the 1982 November sales, I had become very excited about Keeneland and the apparent limitless money available for buying untried yearlings at least eight months before they were even eligible to race.

The heat was already on in the previous July when I was asked by my office to track down Robert Sangster, who had been the major player at the top end. Sangster had been a visionary, in conjunction with Vincent O'Brien, in securing the progeny of Northern Dancer. O'Brien was quick to identify that little horse – winner of the Kentucky Derby – as a stallion of great international potential, following the exploits of Nijinsky, whom he trained for Mr Charles Engelhard. Sangster was to win the Derby with The Minstrel, another Northern Dancer horse, and for a few years – until the Arabs got wind of the supply source – he held sway in Kentucky.

I located Sangster at his hotel in downtown Lexington, and at the end of the 1982 July sale he went through his purchases blow by blow. So helpful had he been that the report which followed was accurate and evocative enough to convince a number of people that I had in fact been at the auction. The experience of talking to Robert, and the subsequent luck to be invited by Keeneland – thanks to the offices of its then chairman James E. (Ted) Bassett, the late Bill Coman and Robin Scully, at whose farm I was generously entertained – was the beginning of a long love affair with Kentucky.

In those early years, Sangster and the Maktoums, supplemented by a number of Saudi owners including Prince Khalid Abdulla and the brothers Prince Fahd and Prince Ahmed Salman, pushed prices to the skies. The process hardly dented the wealth of the Maktoums, although there must have been moments when an element of self-examination took over. It was, though, too much of a high-risk strategy for Sangster.

During the period Sangster enjoyed many major victories, notably the impressive Derby triumph with Golden Fleece. But that horse's misfortunes – he never raced again after Epsom and then died right at the start of his stud career – were big blows. The narrow defeat of his El Gran Senor by Secreto in the Derby was another setback

– although the subsequent Irish Derby victory, allied to his early impressive 2000 Guineas victory, extricated Sangster and the team from a worrying position.

Storm Bird's sale for a reputed £30 million was another triumph; but such was the level of investment in new talent, the strategy required one or more deals of the Storm Bird stature every year, and that was to prove impossible.

History will show the extent of the debt owed to Sangster by British and Irish racing and breeding. A brief list of the other star performers that graced his green and blue colours includes the dual Arc-winner Alleged, Assert (winner of the Irish and French Derbys), Royal Heroine and Turtle Island, as well as the two great stallions Sadler's Wells and Caerleon.

The decision to buy Manton and set up the former champion jumping trainer Michael Dickinson had been pivotal in Sangster's fortunes. Dickinson transformed the place, but a year with just four wins from his team, many of whom were backward youngsters, provoked a split, leaving Dickinson to try his luck in the United States.

The Manton stable then went under Barry Hills' care, before one of Hills' assistants, Peter Chapple-Hyam – who had married Jane Peacock, a step-daughter of Sangster's – was given the job. Classic victories soon arrived for Chapple-Hyam. Rodrigo de Triano, a Sangster home-bred, won both the English and Irish 2000 Guineas, ridden each time by Lester Piggott. That horse was well fancied for the same year's Epsom Derby, but Dr Devious, another Sangster home-bred which had been sold in training to an American couple, won the race.

Less happy moments came with the sales of a number

of Sangster-bred star juveniles, including Balanchine who was later the impressive winner of the Oaks, and most shatteringly of all Cape Verde, five-length winner of the 1000 Guineas. Both these brilliant fillies had passed into the ownership of Godolphin.

At the end of the century Sangster's home-breeding policy did not produce a horse of classic quality, and Chapple-Hyam was replaced by John Gosden. The latter was for a long time a Sheikh Mohammed insider, and overseer of his Stanley House stables in Newmarket. The employment of Gosden, who was bringing a number of his own owners to augment the Sangster horses in Wiltshire, brought full circle the relationships between the two men. When Gosden, a former Vincent O'Brien assistant, started as a trainer in California, among the first to send him horses was Sangster.

There are many in racing who will be hoping that the signing of Gosden, a formidable brain and an open, knowledgeable horseman, will restore the fortunes of the Sangster empire. He deserves to be in the forefront once more.

The Saudis

In the 1980s a large number of Saudi Arabian owners featured on the British turf. Nowadays, the three significant owners from that country are Prince Khalid Abdulla, owner of Juddmonte Farm, his nephew Prince Fahd Salman, who owns Newgate Stud, and Prince Fahd's younger brother Prince Ahmed Salman, who runs his horses under the banner of the Thoroughbred Corporation. All three men have operated at the top level and all have won the most important race in the Calendar for three-year-olds, the Epsom Derby.

HRH Prince Khalid bin Abdulla

In the late 1970s and early 1980s, Prince Khalid operated in the bloodstock markets, acquiring high-class horses, and he has been highly successful throughout the last 20 years. In Dancing Brave he owned one of the best racehorses of the last quarter of the century. Dancing Brave was an unlucky loser of the Derby, but gained a superb triumph in the Prix de l'Arc de Triomphe. The Prince had better luck at Epsom with Quest For Fame and Commander In Chief, the latter a son of his great broodmare Slightly Dangerous, also the dam of Warning.

Warning was a brilliant miler, as was the prince's 2000 Guineas winner Zafonic, whose own son Xaar for a while seemed likely to emulate his father when winning the Dewhurst Stakes so authoritatively. In 1999, Prince Khalid had yet another top-class and unbeaten juvenile in the Dewhurst hero Distant Music. Nowadays, the prince is almost entirely self-sufficient, relying on his exceptional broodmare band to maintain his supply of top-grade horses.

HRH Prince Fahd bin Salman

Although still only in his forties, Prince Fahd has had a long, distinguished career as an owner–breeder, and was responsible for two of the biggest stars of the last decade of the twentieth century. At the start of the decade he was represented by Generous, the impressive winner of both the Epsom and Irish Derbys, and also the King George VI and Queen Elizabeth Diamond Stakes. At the end of the century the prince derived understandable pride from the exploits of his ultra-brave heroine Ramruma, who in 1999 won successively the Epsom, Irish and Yorkshire Oaks. She nearly capped all those achievements when finishing a gallant second in the St Leger, failing only when her stamina was spent in the last 100 yards.

Prince Fahd breeds from a high-class team of mares at his own Newgate Stud, which is run by his manager Anthony Penfold. Every year he is high in the owners' lists, and he typifies the sporting owner for which his country is renowned.

HRH Prince Ahmed Salman

I met Prince Ahmed Salman on my first trip to the July sale in Kentucky. In those days he was barely into his twenties, yet already had won a King's Cup as an owner in his native Saudi Arabia, and had been involved in a number of horses in England.

By that stage he was spending a lot of time in the USA, where he had attended a military college. In this period the prince began an operation called Universal Stables, and was already associated with his long-term trainer Richard Mulhall, a former film stuntman who ran a stable in the backstretch at Santa Anita racecourse, Los Angeles. This was a successful venture, but then the prince returned home to build up his business interests, which includes publishing a group of leading Middle Eastern newspapers.

Then, in 1994, Prince Ahmed renewed the Mulhall

connection, and started his new racing venture, the Thoroughbred Corporation, initially with Mulhall as trainer. A small batch of two-year-olds were acquired that year. Two of them, Supremo and Strong Ally, both were Group 1 placed as juveniles, earning their place in the Breeders' Cup Juvenile – run that year at Churchill Downs, Louisville, home of the Kentucky Derby. Neither horse figured in the big race.

From those small beginnings a major power in world racing was to develop within five years. A first big break-through came when his filly Jewel Princess won at the Breeders' Cup at Hollywood Park, soon followed by a Canadian International success with the three-year-old Royal Anthem, shipped in from Henry Cecil's stable at Newmarket.

A year later the prince was able to look back on an impressive Derby winner in Oath, a Breeders' Cup Juvenile success with Anees, and a superb Juddmonte International victory, by eight lengths, from Royal Anthem. That talented horse then added a third Grade 1 success when, having moved across to be trained by Bill Mott, he collected a major winter race at Gulfstream Park, Florida, in February 2000.

For a short time during the 1999 season Royal Anthem was considered probably the best horse in the world. He was unlucky, however, to have a fully matured and top-form Daylami as an opponent in three other races during the year. In the Coronation Cup and the Breeders' Cup Turf, he followed that champion over the line, while he was out of sorts when unplaced behind the grey in the Irish Champion Stakes.

Royal Anthem, who is sure to be in great demand when he goes to stud, is a half-brother to the prince's favourite, Sharp Cat. That daughter of Storm Cat was a brilliant front-running filly who was one of the best of her age group throughout her career. She probably would have ended with success in the 1998 Breeders' Cup, but she became 'tied-up' after a final piece of work before the Distaff race for which she would have been a firm favourite. For a couple of days Sharp Cat caused great concern that she might not recover, but eventually she was nursed back to full health and has begun a second career in the breeding shed.

As well as his exploits on the track, Prince Ahmed made news with his signing of Gary Stevens as his retained jockey, causing the great American to cut short a visit to England in the late summer of 1999. A few months into the new job, Stevens had to retire from the saddle owing to persistent knee problems. He is now on the management team of the Thoroughbred Corporation, reporting directly to Richard Mulhall.

Prince Ahmed splits his string between the USA and England, where Henry Cecil is his main trainer. In 1998 the prince's Saudi Arabia colours of green and white stripes were carried with consistent distinction by Dr Fong, a horse named after the surgeon who had looked after the prince's mother when she needed medical treatment in earlier years.

The equine Dr Fong proved talented enough to give the prince a Royal Ascot success in the Group 1 St James's Palace Stakes, and was then a highly creditable and closing second to old adversary Desert Prince in the all-aged Queen Elizabeth II Stakes at Ascot. That September Group 1 contest often settles the mile championship of Europe, and so it proved in that year when Desert Prince was officially and quite fairly assessed as one pound the superior of Dr Fong at the top of the tree.

The decision to syndicate Dr Fong and stand him at the Side Hill Stud in Newmarket was so well received that the horse was fully subscribed before the Tattersalls December sale. With Royal Anthem and Anees also in line for stud careers within the next few years, Prince Ahmed Salman is moving to the heart of racing's international big time with rapid strides.

CHAPTER SEVEN

Leading Trainers

On the flat

The favoured image of a top racehorse trainer is of a priv-
ileged, often arrogant man, driving a Mercedes, taking
winter holidays in Barbados and treating his owners as a
necessary evil.

It is easy to take that view, and envious people and betting shop pundits probably do. A more appropriate pen
portrait, at least of those in the top echelon, is of the boss
of a medium-sized business with a turnover approaching
£3 million, who works from dawn until late in the evening. He or she combines the skills of a managing director,
accountant, psychologist (human and equine) and vet,
and still has to satisfy the requirements of a demanding
group of owners at all hours of the day.

The longer I have been around trainers, the more I've
come to admire their industry, adventure, and plain effi-
ciency at what is a highly competitive job. Not only do
they lose in career terms when one of their horses fails
to win as expected, there is also a direct financial cost.
Owners rarely hesitate to move their horses to the latest

fashionable stable when they feel results have been unsatisfactory.

Henry Cecil

Probably the best recent example of a top-flight withdrawal by an owner from a stable was the departure of Sheikh Mohammed's horses from Henry Cecil in September 1995. The ten-times (or nine depending on which basis for calculation you choose) champion trainer has since recovered from what was a serious setback for himself and a shock for the whole of racing.

It was Cecil who had supplied the majority of the sheikh's classic winners up to the latter's departure into the Godolphin experiment – including the fillies' triple crown with Oh So Sharp (1000 Guineas, Oaks and St Leger). The loss of the Maktoum horses was a severe setback, not least that of Mark Of Esteem, the horse whose lameness before a major race objective sparked the rift. Mark Of Esteem went on to win the next year's 2000 Guineas.

Cecil was fortunate to have other leading owner–breeders in the stable, while the continued strong support of three Saudi Arabian princes enabled Cecil to battle back to the top. In 1999 he landed three English classics – the 1000 Guineas with Prince Khalid bin Abdulla's Wince; the Oaks with Prince Fahd bin Salman's Ramruma (who also won the Irish Oaks), and the Derby with Prince Ahmed bin Salman's Oath. In addition, Enrique was second in the 2000 Guineas and Ramruma was heroic when second in the St Leger.

Cecil's methods are not just traditional; they are based

much more on his instinct when looking at horses in the stable than on any of the now routine indicators, like regular weighing and blood analysis. All the modern testing methods are available, of course, but a career which has yielded a record 22 domestic classic wins spanning a little over 30 years would hardly be considered anything other than a framework for the art of training.

Cecil's pattern of working horses differs from that of the two-furlong uphill interval style of training. The sight of Cecil's string setting out for one of the more remote working venues is one of the unchanging images of Newmarket, racing's Headquarters. On either one of the week's two serious work days, the pattern is a template of training. Upwards of 60 horses, with lads and lasses smartly attired, comprise a single 'lot'. First they trot for half a dozen circuits in the spacious indoor school at Warren Place. They are then walked to a collecting point, before cantering down to the start of the gallop.

Cecil's work days always offer excellent material for the racing press, so there is usually a journalist or two waiting close to the trainer as the horses come up to the finish of the gallop. On a good day he will call out the names from the most significant 'sets' in the work, and in the build-up to Guineas week and the Derby the atmosphere is of a really exclusive club.

Owners often attend, and there is nothing quite like having an interest in a Cecil horse which makes it into the first division at the beginning of the year. That was my experience with Hitman, and even though the horse had his problems, it was exciting to follow the exploits of some of those he had smashed in gallops, winning good races later in the year.

Cecil's unfortunate experience with Sheikh Mohammed, and then in 1999 the rift in his second marriage, to Natalie, and the decision to sack Kieren Fallon as stable jockey, all had major effects on this sensitive, private man. Happily, Cecil has become extremely popular with the public, so he drew much satisfaction and comfort during this time. His unfailing charm and politeness make him almost the last real gentleman of the turf in the accepted sense. He is certainly a trainer of the old school. His stepfather, Captain Sir Cecil Boyd-Rochfort, was acknowledged to be the best trainer of Cup horses of his generation.

Cecil's first wife Julie's father was Sir Noel Murless, whom he succeeded at Warren Place, Newmarket. Sir Noel was the outstanding British trainer of the period between 1950 and 1970. Henry Cecil has since become the dominant practitioner of the same art, following similar traditions of preparation and feeding, as his outstanding predecessors.

Sir Michael Stoute

If the aristocratic Henry Cecil had always imagined he would become a great trainer, his close contemporary Sir Michael Stoute could hardly have believed that he would one day be recognised as one of the supreme trainers. Classics, Breeders' and Japan Cups and big wins all around the world have become commonplace for this son of a former chief-of-police in Barbados.

After coming to Britain, Stoute set up a small Newmarket stable, and his skill at preparing rewarding gambles soon resulted in his attracting bigger owners. Where Sheikh Mohammed was the principal Maktoum connection for Cecil, Stoute's mainstay was elder brother Maktoum al Maktoum. The most important springboard, however, was the patronage of His Highness the Aga Khan.

The Aga Khan, the third member in direct line of his family to grace the British turf, heads a small Muslim sect, the Ismailis. His grandfather, also the Aga Khan, owned two triple-crown winners (2000 Guineas, Derby and St Leger) in Mahmoud and Bahram, while his son, Prince Aly Khan, owned the flying filly Petite Etoile.

It is arguable, though, if either of the princes ever possessed a horse with the magnetic appeal of a chestnut colt called Shergar, not just for his brilliance on the race-track, but also for the tragedy that overtook him at almost the start of what proved a criminally short stud career. Stoute brought Shergar along in his usual steady fashion, winning once as a two-year-old, and then winning successively the Sandown Classic Trial and the Chester Vase, the latter by an almost embarrassing margin. With the youthful Walter Swinburn in the saddle, Shergar was overwhelming favourite on Derby Day and won in the desired fashion, by ten lengths. He followed up in the Irish Derby and 'King George' at Ascot to confirm his status. His theft less than two years later, from the Aga Khan's stud on the Curragh, proved a sad finale to his career and life. Shergar was never found again.

Stoute's status has not diminished. He has shown his

skill, especially in handling mature horses, continuing to find improvement into their third and even fourth seasons in training. Both Pilsudski and Singspiel were examples of his facility to continue to develop talent into mature years.

Saeed bin Suroor

One morning in Dubai early in 1995, a group of English and Irish journalists were invited to a press conference, conducted by Sheikh Mohammed. We were there to become more acquainted with the facilities available to horses in the sheikh's embryonic Godolphin experiment, whereby horses spent the winter in Dubai to take advantage of the warm Gulf weather. When the sheikh announced that he had appointed Saeed bin Suroor as Godolphin's trainer, most of those present found it difficult to suppress laughter.

The sheikh explained that this young man, a policeman in Dubai, had impressed him with his training of a small team. He won several races in the developing Dubai racing scene. With such as Simon Crisford, Godolphin's Racing Manager, and Jeremy Noseda to assist him, as well as some excellent staff, many predictably glossed over bin Suroor's part in the achievements of Godolphin, which in 1995 astonished most observers.

The replacement later of Noseda by the American, Tom Albertrani, did nothing to alter the smooth running of the operation, and in subsequent years the quiet, methodical and highly polite and friendly Saeed has become quite a favourite in Britain, especially with the punters. As his grasp of English has improved, Saeed bin

Suroor's place in racing history will not be just as the label which gets official credit for Godolphin's great achievements. His own part, as the Dubaian national at the head of the team, has been increasingly crucial.

Other top trainers

Barry Hills, John Dunlop and Sir Mark Prescott are three more highly dedicated professionals whose skill in maximising the potential of their horses makes them worthy opponents at the highest level. All three have enjoyed many top-grade successes, but at the same time will be happy to win a small race or two with a less talented animal.

David Loder's career is possibly in a transitional stage. His role as trainer of the Godolphin youngsters at the Evry track in Paris will not really be properly assessed for two or three years.

Another trainer entering a new phase in his career in 2000 was John Gosden. His skills could well push forward the Robert Sangster operation at Manton into a more prominent position after a couple of disappointing seasons.

Over the obstacles

While the level of competition in jumping does not compare with that on the Flat, such experts as Martin Pipe CBE, Nicky Henderson, Paul Nicholls and the top two women trainers, Venetia Williams and Mary Reveley, provide a strong backbone to the sport.

Martin Pipe

Martin Pipe, in terms of winners, runners and horses in his Pond House stable in Somerset, has set new standards and a plethora of records in his 28-year career. Son of a bookmaker, Pipe started with a few horses on the same farm, which is now greatly expanded and improved. It must take brilliant organisational skills to find opportunities for upwards of 200 horses, and to keep the various owners – many of whom have only a single horse, or a share in one – happy and visiting the winner's enclosure.

Much of the efficient backroom organisation is carried out by Pipe's wife Carol, whom he met when she ran his father Dave's bookmaking office. Carol is an innovator, and she has been busily compiling a video to show staff what is expected of them in dealing with their horses. The Pipe interval-training method has been adopted by many former traditionalists. Its key is the requirement of getting his horses supremely fit. They seem to be able to find extra when challenged far more often than the horses of anyone else.

The role of Tony McCoy, the stable jockey, and before him Richard Dunwoody and Peter Scudamore, in maximising the superiority in fitness cannot be overestimated. Pipe's skill is to identify the best in whatever arena, and adapt or recruit it. Just the same, no jockey ever carried a horse to win, although no doubt McCoy will probably be doing that one day. It is the fitness of the horses that continues to amaze. Pipe is simply unique, and is also the best exploiter of the jumping programme book. He compares in jumping almost to Sir Mark Prescott's legendary exploitation of Flat race conditions.

Pipe's many Cheltenham successes over the years have not so far yielded a Gold Cup. He and many others believed and hoped that the astonishing novice, the French import Gloria Victis, could fill that gap. How cruel that Pipe and owner Terry Neill, not to mention McCoy and the horse's lass, should be deprived of Gloria Victis's brilliance by his fall, ultimately fatal, in the 2000 Tote Cheltenham Gold Cup.

Nicky Henderson

Nicky Henderson's career has been just as successful as Pipe's in terms of big-race successes, and this trainer – who can point to a hat-trick of Champion Hurdles with See You Then early in his career – clocked up another four Cheltenham Festival winners in 2000. Henderson's horses always seem most effective on fast or good ground, and the ingredient he seems to develop, almost in Flat-race mode, is speed.

Paul Nicholls

Paul Nicholls' arrival on the jumping scene has been welcome in that he has concentrated on steeplechasers almost to the exclusion of hurdlers. His younger horses have light bumper and hurdling campaigns, and only get to be seriously trained when going over fences.

There is method in such specialisation if you can get the right material and school and handle it efficiently. Most of Martin Pipe's best horses have been hurdlers, whereas the Nicholls figures show a predominance of chase wins, where the money is more generous. With horses like Gold Cup winner See More Business, Queen

Mother Champion Chase hero Call Equiname and Arkle Chase winner Flagship Uberalles already on his CV, Nicholls is destined for a long spell at the top.

Top women trainers

Mary Reveley and Venetia Williams have jointly filled the void for female trainers left by the formidable Jenny Pitman's retirement in 1999. Mrs Reveley, a steady accumulator of wins with Flat racers, hurdlers and chasers, was the one major trainer missing at Cheltenham, a venue she clearly dislikes, and a place where her record is unremarkable.

Venetia Williams, however, attacks Cheltenham with the relish of someone who definitely expects to win races. The measured way in which she aimed the novice Samakaan at the Mildmay of Flete Chase in 2000 typified her approach. Venetia learnt her trade with many of the top exponents, including Martin Pipe. Horses like Teeton Mill and Lady Rebecca have shown she is capable of producing a racehorse to win at the highest level.

CHAPTER EIGHT

Leading Jockeys

Most of the leading British-based jockeys in the late 1990s, both on the Flat and over obstacles, were non-nationals. The retirements of Lester Piggott and Willie Carson in the last half of that decade, and the temporary absence of Walter Swinburn, left massive gaps. Only the Scot Richard Quinn can be expected to challenge the supremacy in numerical terms of triple champion Kieren Fallon, an Irishman, and in cash terms of the Italian Frankie Dettori, who has the might of Godolphin at his disposal.

Fallon's route to his three championships was initially through the decision of Henry Cecil to appoint him for the 1997 season. The pair enjoyed many big-race triumphs, but after three 1999 classics together – with Wince, Ramruma and Oath – they parted company over an issue not related to racing. Fortunately for Fallon, a vacancy became available with Sir Michael Stoute, ensuring that this hard-working jockey will continue to be the man to beat for the title.

Fallon's great asset is his strength and will to win. Also, he is a sympathetic rider and horses seem to run for him. As his time at the top level continued, his once rather rustic style also developed, but power rather than poetry is the Fallon method and it looks that way too.

Frankie Dettori remains the single most charismatic person on the British turf, and the young Italian will always be remembered as the man who rode all seven winners on a single important card, on the Saturday of a Festival of British Racing programme at Ascot. The reaction to the achievement was for punters and the non-racing media to expect a similar feat – or miracle – every time Dettori turned up at a major meeting. The sudden success of two championships, and then this Ascot seven-timer, for a while seemed to reduce Dettori's hunger for racing, and he tended to be blasé about some of the lesser days.

By 1999, though, the hunger was back – possibly because, in part, of Dettori's own reaction to some adverse criticism of his riding of Swain in the 1998 Breeders' Cup Classic at Churchill Downs. Dettori seemed to lose control and uncharacteristically gave Swain a very hard ride, after which he seemed to look for excuses for those excesses. A period of contrition followed, but by the following year he was back at a Breeders' Cup and winning with his great ally, Daylami. The adrenalin was flowing again, and cries of 'Come on me' from the jockey rather seemed to underplay Daylami's part in the equation.

In Britain, Dettori is more able to keep control, and there is no better stylist in the saddle. He is a brilliant tactician, too. When, as is often the case with Godolphin horses, he has something in hand, his rides do have almost a poetic quality, such is the economy of effort and elegance from the rider.

Richard Quinn's status as the best of the rest, solidified by his long, loyal period as stable jockey to Paul Cole, finally earned him a top job for 2000, when he was chosen as the replacement for Kieren Fallon at Warren Place. If the original choice of Fallon had surprised many when Cecil appointed him, owing to their obvious differences in temperament, few believe that Quinn will not make the ideal ally for the top British trainer.

Among leading jockeys, Quinn – and his near contemporary, John Reid – have reputations of unblemished honesty, and Quinn has compiled an impressive record over many years. The Cecil job will propel him into a position where he could challenge Fallon for the title, especially if the Irishman collects any riding bans. Quinn rarely gets himself into a poor position in a race, and the Cecil method of training, which does not centre principally on attaining favourable handicap weights, should suit Quinn's style.

Pat Eddery overcame a serious back problem during 1999 to come with a good late finish to the season. The eleven-times champion even resorted to a few rides and winners on the all-weather to clinch his regular century, which he had managed in every season since the early 1970s apart from one year when he rode mainly in Ireland for Vincent O'Brien.

Eddery's professionalism is matched by John Reid, who was another to overcome a serious injury. The emergence of Jimmy Fortune, who will have the additional strength of John Gosden's other owners to add to the existing Manton firepower, makes this young Irishman another contender for a top-three place.

If there were to be a ballot on who deserves to be acclaimed the best Flat-race jockey in Europe, the chance is that the Frenchman Olivier Peslier would get the nod. Peslier's English day-trips were quite regular in 1998, much to the delight of his English agent Dave 'Shippy' Ellis; but the jockey stayed at home much more in 1999, and was rewarded by regaining the French title. Style and opportunism are Peslier's trademarks, and he applies them to a warm, outgoing personality, vastly different from that of many regular riders on the British scene. Peslier's attitude is nearer that of the American Gary Stevens, warm and open during his short 1999 stay at Newmarket.

Opinions on jockeys are plentiful enough. In my association with and period of writing on racing, I have never previously considered that the leading exponents of jump racing would ever compare with their counterparts on the Flat. In the last half of the 1990s, however, a comet appeared, or so we thought. Such was the rapidity of the rise of Tony McCoy, and so harsh were the sanctions that he applied to his own body in the search for excellence, that we expected his lifetime at the top to be brilliant but brief.

We got the 'brilliant' part, but brevity seems to be no more a part of the McCoy strategy than it has been part of his boss, Mr Pipe's. Day after day, McCoy astonishes with his determination; amazes with his will to win, and sometimes dismays us with his uniformly angry reaction to defeat. Year on year, the improvements to his style have been ever more apparent.

McCoy's power, perhaps harnessed more selectively, still overwhelms most opponents. Not only do his fellow jockeys appear almost like rabbits transfixed in the headlights of his excellence, but his mounts are tangibly enforced and enabled to run beyond the limits of their apparent ability. All the components are there, to which you can add an uncanny tactical awareness, and the true horseman's facility to judge a stride at a fence from a long way off.

None of this admiration comes as a result of my winning money backing McCoy horses. I often catch him when a Pipe horse actually runs below par. No, it's the regular experience of finding what looks a good thing, only for a trademark McCoy finish to obliterate any hope of a winning bet. At one stage I even told myself I would never nap (day's best bet) a horse when McCoy was in the opposition.

McCoy is the only jump jockey I will attempt to assess in this section about major players. For all their abilities, Richard Johnson, Mick Fitzgerald, Adrian Maguire and Norman Williamson are relative also-rans, like the top handicappers used to be against Arkle. Arkle was named after an Irish mountain. There is no question that Tony McCoy is at the peak of his profession and will stay there as long as the hunger remains. For my part, I think he is the best jockey, either Flat or jumping, I have ever seen. He's an Arsenal fan, too.

CHAPTER NINE

Track Fortunes

In the old days there was nothing very sexy about owning a racetrack. Fixtures were limited and most race meetings were staged when many people were otherwise engaged. Gradually the increase in evening racing during the summer period enabled more people to attend, and Sunday racing has added another group of potential racegoers to the equation.

Many of the courses, owned by rich local men, offered only modest facilities. Gradually, tracks came under the ownership of fewer individuals, and groups like the Jockey Club-owned Racecourse Holdings Trust built up a big portfolio. RHT, already controlling Newmarket, Cheltenham, Aintree and Haydock among others, during the 1990s added the United Racecourses group. Their three tracks – Epsom, Sandown and Kempton – are close to London and have added an extra metropolitan ingredient to the provincial character of the RHT package.

RHT-owned tracks have inevitably become the prime movers in the Super Twelve grouping which was put together by such as Newmarket's Kim Deshayes, Ascot's Douglas Erskine-Crum and Edward Gillespie from

Cheltenham, to attempt a cohesive approach, especially of future television rights.

While the Racecourse Holdings Trust team has been concentrating principally on domestic issues, some of the other players have been more flexible. Graham Parr of Arena Leisure, for example, correctly predicted that the internet would be a major element in future developments in racing. Parr, an executive for many years in the leisure industry, started in his student days as a bingo caller in his home town of Blackpool. He was soon working with Trevor Hemmings in the Pontins organisation, and many years later persuaded his friend, who was already a major racehorse owner, that horseracing was a field in which there could be large potential earnings.

Parr identified the sport's situation in the late 1990s as similar to that of professional soccer in Britain in the immediate pre-Sky TV era. The influx of cash into football, Parr reasoned, could spill over into racing, given the right conditions. The development of digital television, coupled with interactive betting machines and improved quality of pictures on computer screens via an internet link, would provide those conditions, he reckoned.

In the spring of 1999, the shares of Arena Leisure, the company into which Parr effected a reverse takeover to facilitate the acquisition of Lingfield, stood at 12p. By early 2000 the shares had gone beyond £2.60, before settling around the £2 mark and giving the company a market value of more than £500 million. Richard Muddle – who with father Ron had taken a large tranche of shares as part-payment when Arena bought the Muddles'

Wolverhampton and Southwell tracks – was worth on paper more than £50 million himself.

That level of good fortune for an individual, and the other shareholders, inevitably brought a dash of the favoured British disease, envy. Reports in the *Racing Post* ridiculed a market system that could value a company at more than £500 million when it made a profit of just £2 million. Parr pointed out that the historical profits were based on a widely different marketplace from the future internet-led world market where bets will be paid into pari-mutuel pools.

The imminent withdrawal from controlling racing's funds by the Labour government, announced in March 2000, may have a more significant result even than the discontinuing of the Levy system for funding racing, and the acquisition of the Tote by a racing trust or its like. It could lead to the eventual erosion of the Tote's monopoly position for pool betting in this country. Then Parr – the man with control of 20 percent of all race fixtures in Britain, as portfolio of the three all-weathers, plus Windsor and Folkestone, added to the management of Worcester – will be able to generate rather more profits for his shareholders.

The other lion in the racetrack-owning field is Stan Clarke, whose St Modwen property group provided him with the finance, first to become a racehorse owner, and then a track owner. Clarke was already in control of Uttoxeter and Newcastle when his brilliant chaser, the New Zealander Lord Gyllene, ran away with the IRA-delayed Grand National of 1997. Soon after Clarke added management of both Brighton and Chepstow, but his plan for an all-weather track in addition to the existing turf course at Gosforth Park, Newcastle, was unsuccessful.

Despite this a possible alliance between Arena and the St Modwen tracks owned and controlled by Clarke would give the two groups a balancing potential with RHT, and a larger number of total fixtures. These two men also have toughness acquired in business, so whatever the future for internet betting and broadcasting, they will be major players when the blueprint for the next half-century is laid down.

The chance of one, or even two, entirely new race-courses, the first since 1927, was made possible by the decision of the British Horseracing Board to grant fixtures, subject to satisfactory planning conclusions, to London City and Pembrey for 2000 and beyond.

London City, to the east of London, in Fairlop, proposes 31 floodlit Thursday night fixtures on a dirt surface equating to those in the United States. Pembrey, in an area of South Wales where significant economic regeneration is scheduled, plans 10 turf fixtures. Naturally, much will depend on the feelings of local councils and residents in each area.

CHAPTER TEN

Betting in the New Millennium

The future in vision

Society is moving on. Where once the consumer-led western world was becoming populated by increasing numbers of couch potatoes, in the year 2000 and beyond the next generation will be casting aside their settees and pulling a hard-back chair up to the computer screen.

Instead of being comfortable, and enjoying a leisurely beer and a sandwich while watching his or her favourite soccer team in action (or in the USA, football, baseball, hockey or basketball team), now the punter will be 'surfing' – as we internet-familiar friends of Bill Gates call it. Whether the sport be soccer or boxing, cricket or racing, the chance is that the addict will be able to pursue it either on a digital television screen or on a computer terminal. The truly keen might even keep in touch by watching on a mobile phone while walking along the local high street, possibly re-discovering the now-abandoned pastime of shopping in an actual shop.

The difference between racing and the other sports is that you can have a proper bet. What can you do with soccer? Silly bets on corners, 0.4 of a goal superiority or shirt numbers might appeal for a week or two, but how can you win any proper money? As the 2000 Cheltenham Festival showed – and this is something I've always believed – there is an almost limitless amount of money available for betting. You simply need to provide the most suitable components to encourage people to participate. The hordes of punters who attend any one of the three days at Cheltenham are able to get on anything.

For years, the thing about bookmakers has been that you have what you like, as long as they want you to have it. If anybody doubts the small frame of ante-post punters, and consequently the minute ante-post market, the starting prices for the two overnight favourites in the 2000 Triumph Hurdle would have convinced them. Mister Banjo and Snow Drop were both around the 7-2 mark the day *before* 28 runners went to post. On the day, Snow Drop started the 7-1 favourite and ran out an impressive winner; Mister Banjo was allowed to go off at 9-1 and was unplaced. This demonstrates that a proper spread of bets, as when 50,000 people attend a meeting, by definition and in practice brings better odds.

When worldwide television eventually allows a representative audience, rather than the two artificially curtailed sections we have now, the same will be true. At present, an on-course market dictates the odds in shops, while a small sample of the total number of potential punters bets on the Tote, again providing a weak sample. What might once have been described as a 'grandiose' scheme, for a worldwide 24-hour single stream with multiple choice of several fixtures in different countries running at the same time, is now not only possible but imminent.

The world network could begin with races from Australia and New Zealand; proceed to Japan, Hong Kong and Singapore, thence to Dubai – religious considerations on gambling permitting. South Africa would be the next potential segment, followed by Eastern Europe, Germany, France and Italy, just before the British element kicks in.

Most British daytime fixtures finish around 5 pm, which is noon in New York and time for the first race on the East Coast. The three-hour delay for California brings us almost full circle and time for the Australians to wake up and start the carousel off again.

The key element in all instances is that of *rights*. Once a supplier of pictures is given the rights to the race fixtures of his or any other country's racing, he can get going. The wish for a single combined channel is a worthy one, but there are a number of American companies each holding sections of the rights in their own country and there will be plenty of horse trading before they coalesce.

My bet is that, around 2004, any insomniac in London or Glasgow wishing to do some internet version of counting sheep need only click on to the relevant channel showing racing from the Meadowlands in New Jersey. Unless he is unlucky and chooses a day or night when there is a thoroughbred meeting, he will have the sight of a bunch of trotters or pacers going around the tight little track, with its instant sleep-inducing properties.

The case for scrutiny

The formation of the British Horseracing Board (BHB) left the previously omnipotent Jockey Club with three specific areas of responsibility. Discipline, regulation and security remained under the Jockey Club ambit and those areas have always been the points of potential damage for the image of the sport.

In early 1998, a number of jockeys and other licensed and unlicensed individuals were arrested by the police on suspicion of having been involved in various illegal acts concerning racing. The major points at issue were the alleged doping of two horses, Avanti Express and Lively Knight, and the betting movements relating to each of two events on separate dates in the winter of 1997. Both horses had been well fancied and each ran appallingly. Lively Knight was a long odds-on chance when he was 'got at', and his rider on the day, a young jockey called Leighton Aspell, was one of those arrested, as was Jamie Osborne, who rode Avanti Express in his race.

During a long delay, this pair and three other senior jockeys – Ray Cochrane, Dean Gallagher and Graham Bradley – were forced to suffer while police decided whether to press charges. In the end only Bradley was charged, and even those charges were dropped. No case was brought against any other licensed individual, including the trainer Charlie Brooks.

Others, generally punters, were less fortunate, and some still face the prospect of a trial, which to my mind will be handicapped because of most policemen's lack of understanding of how the betting market works.

It is true that, for one reason or another, a horse might not be fancied. The most simple case is that the animal is a non-trier. If that is so, then the usual indicators and barometers that the security aspect of racing has at its disposal could well uncover such a case.

It only takes a couple of people in the know to start the sort of run, either for or against a horse, that can be equally true when the bush telegraph gets into full stride, for example, in a stock market. If punter A knows that a horse will not win and that he is a short-priced animal, he will either attempt to lay the horse privately, or to have a bet on another horse. This could be the second-favourite, with bookmaker B. Either transaction might be overheard by another punter, say C. He then tells his friend D, a big punter, to step in. In the case of the two doped horses, an element of this sort of 'information by osmosis' could well have been the reason for some of the arrested punters to place their bets.

Racing works on fact and rumour, guesswork and prejudice. The snag, as far as the police goes, is that when they get involved in this aspect of the sport very few will understand that the components of a gamble often start with a small ripple at long odds by one shrewd punter. He can be responsible for initiating a major gamble, in which much of the betting is done, in-house, with one bookmaker laying off with another, all at ever-decreasing prices. That situation is often described as a big gamble, when actually it is not.

The Jockey Club is rightly careful to advance the case

that racing needs to be shown to be as straight as possible. That is true, but there lurks in every unlucky or unsuccessful punter (according to his or her degree of self-deception) the reassuring knowledge that 'the game is not straight'. At least then the punter can justify, personally and to cronies in the local betting shop, why he or she is always losing money on 'good bets'.

Doping, of course, is totally reprehensible, causing the potential for injury to horse and rider, as well as other participants who might get in the way. Dope also has the capacity for destroying animals with ability, so that they may perhaps never perform at their proper level once they have been doped.

Non-triers, as a generic group, have become an endangered species. A jockey attempting to 'bury' a horse, especially one that has an obvious chance on previous form, will have every move monitored by the battery of cameras, some from the technical branch of racing, others from the major networks or the Racing Channel and Satellite Information Services. If that coverage proves inconclusive, the second element is the report of the Betting Intelligence Officer, who stands in the ring watching market movements. Rapid lengthening of the odds about a horse before a race alerts the ring that something may be wrong. The two elements of a drifting horse and a dodgy-looking ride will usually bring a penalty under the non-triers rule.

Discipline for all sorts of infringements comes under the Jockey Club's control. Whip offences, where the jockey tries too hard to win and breaks the rules, deservedly bring fines and suspensions. More serious incidents like doping are a matter for the police and the courts.

Everything considered, however, just where does the responsibility reside for dealing with a case like the one I heard about some years ago? A jockey – who has since done well in racing under Jockey Club Rules – began his career riding in flapping races in his native Wales. This man, who has ridden a winner in my own colours, went up to Scotland one day as a young boy. He rode in a race confined to girls, and won. The 'flaps' in those days were presumably rather less strict than the Jockey Club is now.

CHAPTER ELEVEN

Personal Notes

City road to Canary Wharf

You know you're getting old when the time you have been in a job exceeds the length of your life before you took it. In my case that watershed arrived in 1998, after 26 years at the *Daily Telegraph*. Fifty-four, the age I arrived at in 2000, had for a long time been prevalent in my mind rather than the rounded number which attracted such attention. Reaching those two landmarks has for me had the effect of casting back the mind to earlier times.

Old Etonians, of which there are so many in racing and politics, need only look around the nearest corner to find an old school chum. Old Cowperians – former pupils of the Central Foundation Boys' Grammar School (now comprehensive) on the corner of City Road, by Old Street station on the Northern Line in Central London – are thinner on the ground.

Or at least they were, but recently there has been a rash of Old Cowperians in the public eye. Starting with the sublime, a Parkinson show on television revealed that Martin Kemp, the EastEnders and former Spandau Ballet star, went there several years after I'd moved on. Then came, in no particular order, a quartet which illustrates the eclectic nature of the Cowper Street élite.

A chap called Sid Shaw won the right to sell certain items in his London store, which is called Elvisly Yours. Yes, Sid has made a good living out of Elvis Presley memorabilia. He (Sid, not the Pelvis) was in my school year, as was Gary Jacobs who now operates principally as a radio show host offering advice based on his long experience as a lawyer.

I'm glad that Gary made it in the law. The fact that another Old Cowperian named Mel Stein, this time a year older, also took up the law as his profession is admirable. More famously he became the manager – and therefore by definition chief apologist – for the incorrigible Paul Gascoigne. Incidentally another Old Boy, Len Lazarus, is Gascoigne's accountant.

But the last of the group to make the headlines really was a bit much to stomach. Reading a news story about the black economy, I learned that a committee chaired by Lord Grabiner had made recommendations to Gordon Brown's Treasury department. For years the Lord Grabiner – as the Chancellor insists on calling him – was a leading barrister. Many years before, as Tony Grabiner, he was an erstwhile colleague in the school cricket team, and a true professional in the art of profane mickey-taking. I have no idea where he is lord of, but it would be nice to discover that he had become Lord Grabiner of Well Street Common, Hackney. That's where he used to hone his cricketing skills with a pal called Johnny Loftus, from the Eton Manor boys club, who could keep a football up in the air for half an hour at a time.

For me, in those formative years, playing cricket (for London schools and London boys clubs) and football (for Eton Manor and the school) was combined with visits to Highbury, Lord's and The Oval and various race-courses, to produce a hybrid sporting fanatic. One or two members of that club cricket team had an interest in rac-ing, including Terry Peters, the club captain, and Tom Ford, who was my opening partner. Tom and Terry owned a couple of horses together. The best of them was Petersford Girl, trained by Jacqui Doyle, whom they found via a good friend and neighbour of mine, Roger Anderson.

Tom then struck lucky. In partnership with his City colleague Bob Sansome, they bought Zanay, and in the winter season of 2000 that cheap buy won four races in a row. He completed the four-timer, all over the ten-furlong sand track at Lingfield; in the £55,000 Winter Derby, Zanay showed that Jacqui Doyle was a good trainer.

Luckily, Eton Manor and a very fast bowler called Ken Willson – who worked for the *Daily Mail* for many years and liked the fact that I sometimes made a catch off him standing 30 yards back at slip – led me to the *Waltham-stow Guardian*, where Ken had learned his trade. I stayed for a year, disappearing from journalists' day-release classes for shorthand and several less practical skills to continue my education at Sandown and other points of general interest. Threatened with imminent dismissal, I made a speculative phone call to the Editor of the

Greyhound Express, a national daily devoted to dog racing and published opposite the Old Bailey in Fleet Lane.

It would take a full book to describe the amazing characters inhabiting that place, but suffice to say that they included two brothers who were among the first recruited when the paper opened, as dog tipsters. Neither was great at the writing job, but then, as their claim to fame at the time of their being recruited was that they were employed as painters at Wembley Stadium, that is understandable.

After less than a year at the *GE* as a trainee sub-editor, I took a short break to do a summer holiday job at the *Evening Standard*. Nearing the end of the contract, I got a call from the *Greyhound Express* editor, Abe J. Silver – who sounds like a character from a Marx brothers movie, and who behaved like Groucho – to return as Chief Reporter.

Three years there led to a job on the Press Association's racing desk, where the co-inmates included Jonathan Powell, Tony Morris and a great pal in Ron Magee, a Timeform Old Boy. Again there were some strange characters among the older brigade, but then this was the late 1960s. Betting ring guru and fellow Arsenal fanatic Neale Wilkins was another colleague.

When I joined the *Daily Telegraph*, John Oaksey (still bearing his original name of Lawrence under which he rode so many big winners) and Peter Scott were the incumbents.

John had already been there for 15 years and it's amazing to think that he has worked for the *Telegraph* stable for more than 40 years. John will always be a newspaper hero, not least for one amazing piece on a terrible day of weather and disaster at Cheltenham. He wrote something along the lines of: 'Only two stands blew down at Cheltenham yesterday. The Irish won only two races and only one champion (Lanzarote) was killed.' Working with such luminaries as John and the ever-reliable Peter Scott was never dull.

Other colleagues on the desk were the Racing Editor Bob Glendinning, who sadly died in 1999, and his co-Yorkshireman deputy Noel Blunt, another highly memorable man who would rather do a good turn than a bad one. Even ten years after he left his job as News Editor on the much-missed *Sporting Life*, Noel was still remembered with affection, not least for a string of wonderful malapropisms. Many passed us by at the *Telegraph*, but one I love concerns the day when the race titles on a Newcastle jumping card commemorated bird names, with the Eider Chase as the feature. Noel's headline talked about a horse which would 'scale the Eider' – a compelling thought.

I have also to re-tell a tale of the day when one of John Oaksey's pieces stumped Noel, John O'Carroll and Jim Bailey, the team handling the *Sunday Telegraph* desk one Saturday afternoon. Jim asked: 'What are kruggerands?' but neither Noel nor John – whom later it transpired had a few of the gold South African coins which had been in vogue at the time – could help. Noel, spotting me on an adjacent desk where I was subbing football results, had an inspiration. 'Ask Tony,' he said, 'he knows Latin.' Noel it was who got me my job on the desk, and probably helped me keep it in the days when my idea of a break was three races in Corals. Within a short time I'd somehow fluked it to Racing Editor, a job that exactly spanned the same period that Mrs Thatcher occupied Downing Street.

The nice thing about that time was the fact that several people joined our team on my recommendation. Adrian Hunt, Kevin Perry, Mike Roberts, Steve Dillon and Brian Matthews all came that way, as did my original deputy, Howard Wright, who now stars as a fount of industry knowledge on the *Racing Post*. George Hill, my big pal, left to become a bloodstock agent and has many good winners, and a few that got away, on his curriculum equus.

The only one still at the *Telegraph* on the inside staff who escaped my net was Danny Coupland. He had the distinction of being employed directly by the Sports Editor, Kingsley Wright, another doyen of the old Fleet Street, and yet another Yorkshireman. Danny never once threatened to prove the Old Boy wrong, and like the rest of the inside team has eased my job and those of Jim McGrath, Marcus Armytage and our new star Richard Evans.

The irascible Wright was completely different from the present Sports Editor. David Welch had the foresight to bring out the first sports supplement in a national newspaper as long ago as March 1990, giving a lead in sports journalism which the paper has never relinquished. He is also a racing fan, which makes it at once easier and harder to work for him. You won't get a rubbish piece past him, but he knows a good story when he sees it. (I'll write one before long, David, I promise – probably when you agree to go to an all-weather meeting.)

Trainers and Owners

The first dabble I ever had with a horse was a long time ago. It must have been, because he won a race at Lanark, which has been closed for a quarter century, and the trainer Louie Dingwall was already in her late seventies.

Old ma Dingwall ran a scruffy little stable, and a petrol pump, close to the beach at Sandbanks, near Poole in Dorset. She was a funny old dear; but like Red Rum and Ginger McCain, her horses loved the beach and the saltwater did wonders for the legs of the sort of patched-up old crocks she had to train.

Mrs Dingwall decided one day to drive her box down to the South of France. In it was an old horse called Treason Trial. This was the 1970s when the Dingwall horses would be running for prizes of a thousand or two at most. Treason Trial travelled down to Nice to run at the lovely track at Cagnes-sur-Mer, and blow me if he didn't win the Grand Prix des Alpes Maritimes, the most important race of the early season at Cagnes. It carried a purse of £15,000. I can still hear Mrs D saying: 'Well my dear, that was all right, wasn't it?'

She bought Princehood at a sale for 260 guineas. The animal, which had a good pedigree, was by the sprint sire Princely Gift, and was out of a decent mare, Green Halo, a daughter of the Queen's top-class racehorse Aureole. He had won first time out for Atty Corbett's stable, but then ran badly twice – hence his cheap price. On seeing the sale return in the *Sporting Life*, I rang her and she agreed to sell him to our ten-strong syndicate comprised mainly of *Telegraph* sub-editors. It was £50 a shot. Eventually he left

Poole for Ken Payne's stable at Middleham, now the base of Mark Johnston, and won us a BBC televised race, the Royal Scots Dragoons Guards Cup, at Lanark. He started at 14-1 and broke the five-furlong track record, called home by the dulcet tones of Julian Wilson, drowned out in the Kings and Keys public house, Fleet Street, on that Saturday by a number of syndicate members.

Incidentally, from a small staff at Sandbanks, future trainer Paddy Butler, Joan le Brocq, who trains in Jersey, and the other Peter Scott all emerged. This Peter, a Geordie, is nowadays confined to a wheelchair, but is the proud owner of the tough filly Diamond White, winner of the 1999 Prix de l'Opera on Arc day at Longchamp. They have all achieved more than is usual for a stable lad. To complete the team, there was the stylish Flat and jumping jockey and noted deckchair stacker Gary Old, who preferred the girls on the beach to the horses in the summer.

Working at the *Daily Telegraph* was always interesting and you could never anticipate what might happen next. Having started an extra job as part-time editor of the weekly racing paper *The Racehorse*, I had a call one night in Fleet Street from Michael Dickinson – who, it seems, was a regular reader. The paper had a number of regular columnists, such as Roger Mortimer, formerly of the *Times*, and Howard Wright, who was just as accurate and economical in his writing style even in those far-off days.

There was also a column written from France by a great friend, Prince Rajsinh of Rajpipla, an Anglo-Indian who had owned horses in his late teens and was a friend of the social set which included a very young Joan

Collins. The Prince's father, the Maharajah of Rajpipla, had owned the Derby winner Windsor Lad, before Pippy was born. Pippy had been one of the pioneers in buying horses from France, and was in the same stable, that of Peter Cazalet, in which the Queen Mother's horses were housed. Pippy sold a couple of his better ones, Oedipe and Three No Trumps, to her.

Eventually it was Pippy who suggested to me that Michael Dickinson and his father Tony might do better buying from France than Ireland. The result was a deal in which they acquired French Hollow, from the British-born owner Malcolm Parrish, who at the time operated a big stable in Chantilly. French Hollow was a classy Flat-race handicapper who won a string of high-grade novice hurdles for the Dickinsons before being sold on to steeplechase in America, where he again did very well.

Apart from regular calls to the *Telegraph*, usually after a couple of hours at the sauna (this was in his riding days), Michael also kept in touch with Walter Glynn, a comment writer for the *Raceform* form book, and another contributor to *Racehorse*. In those days there was rather less risk of being sued for libel, which was fortunate for Glynn, his editor and publisher, so strong were some of his comments concerning non-triers as he had assessed them. Of course he was right, more often than not.

Michael Dickinson still maintains – after two Breeders' Cup Mile wins with Da Hoss, not to mention his achievement of saddling the first five home in a Gold Cup, and 12 winners on a single Boxing Day – that he learned the handicapping of races from me. I wish I could have picked up training horses from him!

I can claim one triumph. At the time of our regular contacts, I bombarded Michael with pleas for him to buy a three-year-old out of the Luca Cumani stable. That horse, called Honnegger, was not very big, but I saw him win a race one day at Redcar with a display of such courage that convinced me he'd make a jumper. I think he won 18 races. Then again, I'm sure there are 18 other horses I've recommended to owners and trainers that have not won a race between them.

Ireland has some interesting bookmakers, even if J. P. McManus no longer needs to stand on a joint to make ends meet. One of his compatriots, who succumbed early to Hodgkin's disease, was the tough Belfast-born Sean P. Graham, whose sons Sean Jnr and Brian now operate the business he built up with great energy in the 1970s.

One day, Sean suggested I speak to a trainer of his. That led to my meeting Jim Bolger, a trainer whose skills and capacity for hard work not only secured his own place among the top trainers of his and any other country, but rubbed off on two of racing's greatest young stars. Both Aidan O'Brien and Tony McCoy started with Bolger, and there is no disguising the man's trademark on his young protegees.

My first call to Jim was met with a brief silence, followed by: 'Now you won't be mentioning any [horses'] names, will you? We'll both know who you're talking about.' For a long time we had a close connection, and there were few trainers better able to exploit tough, cheaply bought fillies than Jim. Once he took a selling-plater, My Hollow, from an English hurdle race and turned her into a group-winning filly. From then and up to his triumphs with St Jovite, in the Irish Derby and 'King George', and Jet Ski Lady in the Oaks, he showed and continues to show that he can operate at the highest level.

I met St Jovite's owner, Mrs Virginia Kraft Payson, in Kentucky and have been friendly ever since with her and her son Dean Grimm. On the night of St Jovite's 'King George' we were looking for a location for the celebration party. In the end we managed only to get a table at San Lorenzo in London, when Mrs Payson agreed to bring in the trophy and allow it to reside in splendour on the table.

On my initial visit to Kentucky, my host Robin Scully took me to the Hyatt hotel. It was a Sunday and in those days Kentucky was dry. We sat with two other men at a table. The first was Peter Brant, a polo-playing owner, who made his money in newsprint. He heard of my *Daily Telegraph* connection and said: 'You know, if the British newspapers could sort out the unions, they would be among the biggest money-spinners in the world.' Brant still regrets, or says he does, not taking up my suggestion to buy the paper.

The second gentleman at the table was one of those characters you meet only once or twice in a lifetime. Henryk de Kwiatkowski was Polish-born, and his family were wiped out at the beginning of the Second World War. He came to live in England and was under-age when joining the Royal Air Force. On leaving the forces he lived for a while at Dolphin Square, Millbank, before emigrating to Canada, where he worked for the Pratt & Whitney and Sikorsky helicopter companies. Eventually he moved to New York and got into aircraft leasing, in which he made a sufficient fortune to become a major owner–breeder.

The day after our first meeting, when his amazing Hollywood smile first revealed itself, we were together at the sales and he paid a world record 3.8 million dollars for a mare in foal to the great Northern Dancer. Unfortunately he did not buy the foal insurance, and the mare lost the foal and cost him at least a couple of million dollars.

Kwiatkowski, later to become owner of the great Calumet Farm across the road from Keeneland and Lexington airport, was buying mares at that time to be mated with his champion, the Belmont Stakes winner Conquistador Cielo. That night, celebrating with a cup of tea, he predicted greatness for the sire, something which never materialised. As an afterthought he said: 'I have another stallion, whose first runners will race next year. If you have a mare, you can breed her for free.'

That stallion was Danzig, a colt that Henryk raced and which was retired with injury after three easy wins. Even now, half-blind in one eye and totally so in the other, Danzig is still one of the leading stallions, who at one time commanded fees of a million dollars per cover. I didn't have a mare with me at the time, unfortunately.

That initial trip was probably the biggest good fortune of my professional life and entirely due to the recommendation of David Hedges, who sadly died early. David was the European representative of the Keeneland sales company and each year put forward one English journalist who might benefit from a sponsored trip.

Many of the friends and acquaintances I have made in racing have emanated from the Keeneland sales ring. You can take time to talk with some of the leading players in the world's bloodstock business when they are relaxed, rather than at the track, where they tend to be anxious about the imminent running of their horse.

An unlikely footnote is that a few years ago after that first visit to Kentucky, I played in a racing press cricket team and batted together with Annie Hedges, David's daughter, who actually scored some runs.

Rod Simpson is a trainer who has been through the mill and round the track half a dozen times. Even now, in his late fifties he still keeps going, as long as there's a stable to work from and a man to employ him. Rod was always a good stableman, and over time he has made a reputation of being a hard grafter who deserves a bit of luck.

Rod trained one very good horse for me in Tangognat, who won twice at Kempton on the Flat, by 20 lengths and 15 lengths in the same week, and then twice over jumps as a juvenile, each time at Cheltenham, although not in the Triumph Hurdle. One distinction he has given me is that these were the only two occasions that Peter Scudamore had ever ridden in my 'Arsenal' colours of plain red with white spots on cap. Two out of two was the score and both at Cheltenham, if you please. I am convinced that Tangognat would have won the 'Triumph' also had the ground been soft.

That season, I had conducted a package deal on several horses from France, rekindling the Malcolm Parrish connection that had yielded French Hollow for Michael

Dickinson. Rod started to train them, and one of them, Brunico, soon looked a potential star. He was to run for that great character, Terry Ramsden, in the 'Triumph' and finished fast in second. Two months later he won the Ormonde Stakes at Chester at 33-1. Sadly, after Ramsden had been forced out of racing, Brunico became a prolific winner in point-to-points, before meeting an unhappy end after someone attacked him in a field.

In that same Triumph Hurdle there was another former Parrish horse, called Santopadre. Rod had called me one day saying that he had been messing about on the gallops and 'wants shooting'. I had previously met a Durham sheep farmer called Wilf Storey, who struck me as the type of small trainer who might turn him around. Wilf, having informed me that 'no, I don't have anyone with two grand to buy him', agreed to train Santopadre. He ran first time in a seven-furlong race and showed plenty. Then it was decided to get him ready for a hurdle race.

Despite being a little short of work he won that race at Hexham, getting up in the last stride, and followed up in a better seller at Newcastle. When he won by 15 lengths under a double penalty at Wetherby in a decent novice race, he proved to be worth a bit more than two grand. He was just behind the placed horses when fifth in the 'Triumph', running in the Ramsden colours, and the following year was caught in the closing stages of the County Hurdle.

Wilf has been a good friend and contact for all the years in between, so I was delighted when another horse I found for him and his owner, David Batey, broke his duck at the festival. That horse, a son of Caerleon owned by Robert Sangster, was called Great Easeby. He had shown nothing at Manton, and was cheaply bought in a private deal. Wilf brought him along steadily and it was great when, under a superb ride by the seven-pound claimer Richard McGrath, he won the race. We had to wait for a stewards' inquiry before he was confirmed the winner, and we are all still grateful to David Nicholson, whose horse Pharanear had been bumped by Great Easeby, for doing everything he could in the stewards' room to help the result stand.

Another chance call, this time at home, proved equally significant. David Loder, who was just getting going in the Sefton Lodge stables that had housed horses owned by the late Charles St George, asked for my help. He had been recruited the previous winter by Charles' brother Edward, who gave him the chance to go out on his own, thus leaving his job as assistant to Geoff Wragg. He started with a medium-sized team, and a large degree of confidence, so it was a surprise when the call came.

David told me that he was a little worried as his expectations about a few horses had not materialised on the track. He felt concerned that St George might believe he was not up to the job. 'I know that these horses are good, but they keep getting beaten, could you help me with their placing?', David asked. My role proved to be only slightly more than that of a supporter. Immediately his luck changed, the horses started winning, and within months David Loder was the young sensation. Group 1 wins and a few champions in the next few years, by which time my role was entirely that of a non-participating fan, and his eventual signing by Sheikh Mohammed to train exclusively for Godolphin, were only what this talented young man deserved.

Loder's successor at Sefton Lodge was Jeremy Noseda. He is another talented young man and was among the original English recruits when Godolphin first set up its Dubai operation. Since leaving Godolphin after the year of Lammtarra's great triumphs, he gained experience in California in his own right, before buying Paul Kelleway's Newmarket stable. Sadly Kelleway, another character and father of trainers Gay, Anthony and Sara (who trains Arabian racehorses, a separate code) died within a year of retiring to Spain. Noseda soon produced a number of smart horses, and guided the tough Wannabe Grand to second place in the 1000 Guineas of 1999. Even though he is a Spurs fan, I will be happy to see Jeremy break into the big league before long.

A slightly more expensive buy than Great Easeby, at Tattersalls 1996 October Yearlings sale, was Hitman. He was son of the stallion Contract Law, whose move to the Helshaw Grange farm of the talented Richard Kent I had arranged earlier that year. I would not have gone through with that without the encouragement of George Hill. Within a few weeks, George had persuaded the owners of about twenty mares to send them to the stallion, and the exercise proved a success, not least for introducing us to Richard.

Hitman was a good-looking, heavily built colt, and I was very excited when Henry Cecil agreed to train him. Henry's name on the end of the leading rein was enough to convince Peter Mines, who runs the Jet Stationery Co., to form a syndicate. Peter roped in his father Tom, still active in racegoing in his eighties, together with business associates Chris Lee and Peter Tilley, and with me we formed the Paper Boys syndicate.

Being involved with the horse coincided with my taking an interest in the Cecil-trained Thoroughbred Corporation string, for which Willie Carson is European manager. Hitman was looked after by Eddie Cuthbert, like Carson a Scot, and a tough one too. Eddie won five stable lads' boxing titles and even had the formidable Stephen (Yarmouth) Dibble, who was heavier, on the floor before losing that final on points. Eddie is Henry's number two head lad behind the amiable Manchester United fan (can there be such a thing?) Frank Conlon. Eddie is both a shrewd judge and an excellent work rider.

Hitman had cost £11,000 as a yearling, and even though he suffered an inconvenient injury which prevented him from running as a juvenile, as a three-year-old he won in track record time at Newmarket over ten furlongs. He followed that with a fine third place to dead-heaters Rabah and subsequent St Ledger winner Nedawi in Goodwood's Gordon Stakes.

Injury struck again in the Great Voltigeur on his only other start as a three-year-old. Then, after a year and a bit off, he returned with a very disappointing jumps debut at Kempton. Just days after his new trainer, Mark Pitman, entered him for the Champion Hurdle, he was found to have a hairline fracture of the pelvis and taken out of training for a third time.

Such disappointments are the staple diet for all owners, and are never easy to bear. In 1998, I bought another

Contract Law colt, for a Sussex owner, Mike Morley. He was called Move On, and he had been working as well as any of Henry Cecil's better juvenile colts. One day in September the news came that he had broken a leg when doing a routine canter on the gallops and had to be instantly destroyed. Mike was there to see it happen, just days before the colt was due to make what was expected to be a winning debut. Still, when Mike recovers from that experience, like everyone else who has ever owned a racehorse and enjoyed its beauty and the majesty of its power and grace, he'll be back again.

I brushed briefly on my friendship with Prince Ahmed bin Salman and the small part I have in the Thoroughbred Corporation in this country. Without any exaggeration, it is only because of the efforts of another larger-than-life character that this exciting connection occurred. All the major Arab owners have an itinerant entourage, and Jack Rusbridge is the focal point of the Thoroughbred Corporation. Now past retirement age, he retains amazing youthfulness and an inner serenity backed by the knowledge that he can cope with anything.

In his earlier days, Jack served as a physical training instructor in the SAS and boxed as an amateur. He won 300 and lost five bouts in that career, sparring with many of the greats of the 1950s and 60s including Willie Pastrano and Freddie Mills. Jack travels the world, but wherever he is he moves mountains to learn the result of the National Lottery, football pools and anything else that will make a difference to his life. Should he win the lottery he would be able to have even more Superfectas, Trifectas and Pick Six's in partnership with his American pal Dean Shazer, on his trips across the Atlantic. Dean is a native of Pittsburgh, looks like the actor Paul Sorvino and his accent is unlike that of any American I've ever met. As for Jack , he is the most loyal friend and the prototype of the resourceful Cockney, who occurs far more often in fiction than fact.

Grateful thanks are also due Saleh Hammadi, a good friend who arranged my first visit to Saudi Arabia. Saleh is a well-known local media personality and respected not only for his journalistic skills – nowadays he is Editor-in-Chief of a major publication – but also as a noted commentator on soccer. He used to commentate in English on the weekly race meetings, on the country's second television channel. Saleh is an owner and breeder in Riyadh and advises many of the local owners among the Royal family.

For a few guineas more

To end this brief piece of self-indulgence, I have to mention the one that got away. Just three months before acquiring Hitman, I was asked by a Middle Eastern owner to look through the July sale at Newmarket for a horse that might be suitable to run in stayers' races in Saudi Arabia. After putting up a few names, we settled for a gelded son of Sadler's Wells, who had already done well at up to two miles, and I had some first-rate information from John Durkan, then assistant trainer to John Gosden.

We had a rough idea of the budget, and when the client called I started bidding. I stayed in until 36,000 guineas, but when the opposition bid 38,000 we cried off. That horse was triple Champion Hurdle winner Istabraq, and the buyer was Timmy Hyde.

Later it emerged that John Durkan, who had been so honest in not putting me off the horse, was to start training, with Istabraq as one of his first horses. J. P. McManus was the owner, but it soon became clear that Durkan would not be able to take up his appointment, as he had contracted leukaemia, from which he died the following year.

I cannot claim to have known John Durkan well, but I knew him well enough to stop and have a brief word from time to time at the track or on the Newmarket gallops. That episode has left me happy on two scores. I had touched a brief acquaintance with a man of stature, who deserved better than he got. I am even happier that the horse which was to become the best hurdler of the last quarter-century was given the chance that he merited.

A postscript came on a return flight from Kentucky to London in July 1999. Walking between the local and international termini, I was joined by Timmy Hyde, Paul Shanahan and Clem Murphy, who had been at the sale with the Coolmore team. Timmy came alongside and asked: 'You were the underbidder on Istabraq, weren't you?' I answered in the affirmative, adding that it wasn't my money. Timmy continued: 'It's just that ******* Danny Murphy has been quoted in the press that he was the underbidder, but I know it was only you and me for a long while, as I was stood just behind you.' That's the difference between a pro and an amateur – he knew who the opposition might be.

In order to reassure myself that one more bid might have sufficed, I asked Timmy: 'How high would you have gone?' He replied: 'I don't know, but we did think he'd be at least £60,000.' So far yet, apparently, so near.

Index